Theoshini Hitchcock.

ST ANTONY'S COLLEGE, OXFORD

PUBLICATIONS
NO 6

THEORY AND WORLD
POLITICS

St Antony's College concentrates on research in modern history and social studies, with centres or groups specializing in Europe, Russia, Africa, the Middle East, the Far East and Latin America. This new series is an expansion of *St Antony's Papers*, twenty-two volumes of which have appeared since 1956. It is designed to present a selection of the work produced under the auspices of the College, and it will include full-length books and monographs as well as collections of shorter pieces.

previously published

Theory
and
World
Politics

ROBERT J. LIEBER
University of California, Davis

London · George Allen & Unwin Ltd
Ruskin House   Museum Street

ISBN 0 04 320086 9 Hardback
     0 04 320087 7 Paperback

Printed in the USA

FOR NANCY

Contents

4. Cybernetics and Communications Theory   68

5. International Power and Conflict   88

6. Systems Theory   120

Preface

This monograph deals with an array of important new approaches that aim at developing a more reliable and systematic understanding of international relations. It is not my purpose here to recapitulate the elaborate scholastic debates of traditionalists versus behavioralists, nor to categorize the numerous commentaries and criticisms of the various approaches; rather it is my intention to concentrate on presenting a selection of some major new ideas together with a discussion of their possibilities and limitations.

The aim is to illuminate some of the more complex theories and methods, and to do so without losing the reader in a maze of social-scientific jargon. The sometimes impenetrable language used by a number of practitioners of the new approaches has made their ideas less accessible than they would otherwise have been and caused a certain measure of out-of-hand rejection of the ideas in frustration at their presentation. In many cases the use of jargon reflects a self-conscious effort to construct and employ a specialized social science vocabulary with precise meanings; in others it is a sign of unclear thinking, fashionability, sanctification, or even obfuscation. It is true that much of the work in this field has been presented with clarity and considerable explanatory skill, and also that the newer approaches often involve theoretical constructs which, because of their complexity and unfamiliarity, require an added measure of sustained attention from the reader; nonetheless, it is by no means rare to encounter advanced students and even established scholars in international relations who will privately admit their inability to read or understand considerable amounts of recent writing in the field. Although some of the recent work is in fact of dubious value, and the possibility has been raised in relation to individual efforts that "the Emperor has no clothes," [1] a substantial portion of this material possesses considerable worth. Therefore these approaches deserve assessment on their own merits, and it is hoped that the treatment here will provide such an opportunity.

The essays deal with systems theory, communications theory, integration theory, game theory, and ideas about power and conflict. They also offer an assessment of the possibilities of scientific international relations theory and the place of values in this enterprise. Because the book is not meant to be comprehensive, it necessarily omits a variety of approaches, such as theories of decision making and foreign policy making, deterrence theory, economic models, theories dealing with the relation between domestic and international politics, and techniques such as simulation.

With this kind of book, and in the context of the protracted and occasionally vitriolic disputes over what constitutes the most suitable method for the study of international relations, it seems appropriate to summarize my own attitude at the start. Briefly, my theme is that scientific international relations theory is theoretically possible, and that some fascinating techniques, areas of inquiry, and elements of theory already exist, but that in practice, such an achievement remains in its early stages. The best of the contemporary approaches, therefore, have a value that is basically heuristic; that is, they are mainly useful in stimulating our thoughts and in generating new ideas and lines of inquiry. It is in this spirit that the present theoretical introduction to this vast subject is offered, with the hope that it will suggest new possibilities of description, explanation and prediction for all those with interests in international relations.

By way of acknowledgement, I have gained a great deal from the professional influence of Hans J. Morgenthau, Henry Kissinger, Stanley Hoffmann, and Morton H. Halperin, but my most important intellectual debt is to Karl Deutsch, whose insights and arguments in setting out the very real possibilities and advantages of systematic international relations theory I have found so compelling. He would, however, disagree with a number of my overall judgments, particularly as to the actual progress of international relations theory at the present moment.

A number of important suggestions about this manuscript have

[1] Oran Young, "Professor Russett: Industrious Tailor to a Naked Emperor," *World Politics* 21 (April 1969): 486–511.

been thoughtfully offered by Donald Rothchild, Nancy I. Lieber, William W. Bingham, and Steven L. Spiegel. In addition, portions of the work have been read and commented upon by Larry L. Wade, Alexander Groth, Randolph Siverson, Kenneth Hanf, Thomas Westerdale, and M. David Gordon. I also owe a debt to students at Harvard University, the University of California at Davis, and Oxford University for their persistent comments and challenges. I am grateful to Theodore Zeldin of St. Antony's College and David Croom of Allen & Unwin for suggesting that I write this book, and to Jim Murray of Winthrop Publishers for his cooperation. I have benefited from all these counsels, but, ultimately, matters of judgment, emphasis, and conclusion remain very much my own.

1

The

Possibilities

of

Theory

I. Why Do We Need a Theory of International Relations?

Shortly before his death, the late Bertrand Russell spoke of the folly and savagery of warfare and attributed its occurrence to the wickedness and stupidity of statesmen.[1] Former President Harry S Truman offered a rather different explanation for the existence of conflict; in 1957 he stated that "there are some people—and I regret to say some governments—who have not yet accepted the fact that but for Russian intransigence the world would now be enjoying the pursuits of peace."[2] Another approach was that of Lenin, who anticipated that, in contrast to the conflict among states caused by the dynamics of imperialism, communist states would enjoy harmonious relationships based on international proletarian solidarity. And from still another perspective, Woodrow Wilson saw self-determination and democratic government as the means to international peace. These views, each based on an implicit conception of international relations, span the greater part of this century. They reflect the fact that most statesmen view the world from a definite perspective, whether inchoate and unexpressed or precise and explicit. Similarly, most people who observe

---

[1] Filmed interview, shown as part of a television eulogy. BBC–1, London, 3 February, 1970.
[2] *New York Times,* April 28, 1957, quoted in Kenneth Waltz, *Man, the State and War* (New York: Columbia University Press, 1965), p. 157.

world events also have such notions, which enable them to make sense of the subject, though these views are not often clearly formulated and expressed. In short, there have always been "theories" of international relations.

It has been observed that "there is no more vicious theorist than the man who says, 'I have no theory; I just let the facts speak for themselves'." [3] The problem is that some kind of theory (or conception or viewpoint) inherently determines *which* facts are selected, how they are ordered, and in what manner they are interpreted. There is a self-evident need for greater theoretical reliability in our treatment of international relations, yet the above-mentioned notions based on goodness versus wickedness, anti-communism, and Marxism fall quite short of providing satisfactory reliability. Nor is "common sense" sufficient in itself; its notions are often vague or contradictory (cf., "absence makes the heart grow fonder" versus "out of sight, out of mind"). And deep thought alone does not necessarily carry us very far either, for one generation's certainties are often overturned by the succeeding generation. Misperception in international relations repeatedly occurs, whether from faulty information, a difference of perspective, or because a certain viewpoint corresponds to ideological or national needs. Unfortunately, the judgments of policy-makers, based on misleading kinds of information as well as on selective perception, often have proved disastrous. Karl Deutsch notes a number of such examples, as when the Russians obtained their information on the morale of the Finns from Finnish émigré Communists, then ran into unexpectedly stiff resistance when they attacked Finland in 1940; or when General Douglas MacArthur predicted (presumably from introspection) in late 1950 that the Chinese would not enter the Korean War as United Nations forces neared the Yalu River border between North Korea and China. As a more recent example, we may consider the decision of the United States Government to initiate full-scale bombing of North Vietnam. When, in late 1964, the air-strike planners had presented their plan for bombing and asserted that six weeks of

---

[3] Charles O. Lerche, Jr., quoted in Abdul A. Said, *Theory of International Relations* (Englewood Cliffs, N.J.: Prentice-Hall, 1968), p. 1. Also see Karl W. Deutsch, "The Limits of Common Sense," *Psychiatry* 22 (May, 1959): 105–12, reprinted in Nelson Polsby, Robert A. Dentler, and Paul A. Smith, eds., *Politics and Social Life: An Introduction to Political Behavior* (Boston: Houghton Mifflin, 1963), pp. 51–58.

this punishment would surely drive the North Vietnamese to the conference table, one participant in the decision finally asked what would happen if somehow the North Vietnamese did not, after this period, come crawling to the Americans for peace talks. The answer was: In that case another four weeks of bombing would surely do the trick.[4]

In an effort to provide a greater reliability of understanding, political science has, during the last two decades, evolved toward a somewhat more systematic pattern of inquiry about the substance of politics. As a part of this movement, the study of international relations has been increasingly subjected to new types of analysis. Many of the new theories and methods aspire to what has been labeled a *scientific* approach. To the extent that it may be possible, the virtue of such an approach is that it seeks to create knowledge that is impersonal, retraceable and cumulative. If knowledge is impersonal, then Americans and North Vietnamese, Israelis and Arabs, or Indians and Pakistanis are all forced to acknowledge that water freezes at 32° Fahrenheit, or that bodies of gas behave in precise ways under specified conditions of temperature and pressure. And if knowledge is retraceable and cumulative there is no need for slowly and painfully collected insights and discoveries to perish with their discoverers and to be reacquired arduously by those who come after. Because of its formal rationality, science makes our knowledge collective so that others can repeat it.

It is the purpose of these essays to discuss a number of relatively new theories and techniques that offer considerable promise. If we acknowledge the fact that we are bound to approach the subject of international relations with at least some rudimentary theoretical notion, then the question is: Which theory or approach (or combination of approaches) ought we to utilize in this study? The argument presented here is that by adopting some of the newer insights, techniques and theories of contemporary political science we can at least hope to improve the reliability of our knowledge and understanding about international relations.

---

[4] James C. Thompson, Jr., "How Could Vietnam Happen?" *The Atlantic* (April, 1968), p. 51, cited in Richard Pfeffer, ed., *No More Vietnams? The War and the Future of American Foreign Policy* (New York: Harper & Row, 1969), p. 27. See also Theodore Draper, *Abuse of Power* (New York: The Viking Press, 1967), p. 71.

X Also concerned merely z change.

II. The Uses of Theory

In an age of nuclear weapons, the Middle East conflict, Vietnam, civil war in East Pakistan, the Sino-Soviet-American confrontation, and problems of nationalism, communal antagonisms and underdevelopment, the critical nature of international problems is self-evident. Not only are these problems urgent, but they have a direct effect upon us. In the United States, international relations (in the form of the Vietnam war) was recently the leading cause of death among young men in the 15–34 age group. As for the United Kingdom, although few of her soldiers have died as a result of *foreign* conflicts during the last few years, there has been substantial loss of life in Northern Ireland. International events also exercise an immediate effect on Britain's highly sensitive economy, and British possession of nuclear weapons and participation in NATO assure her of involvement in almost any East-West confrontation.

Before we can even consider doing anything about these problems, we must have a certain reliability of understanding. That is, comprehension must precede control. Some of the new theories and techniques set out in these essays do in fact promise marked improvement in our understanding of why and how conflict occurs and how it can be mitigated. In a sense, there is nothing so practical as a good theory,[5] for theory, whether sought for practical application or merely to clarify thinking about international relations, enables us to rise above observation of specific events and it offers us understanding of sequences or patterns of occurrences.

For whom is this improved understanding of international relations to be of use? Some recent criticisms of contemporary scientific, or behavioral, approaches have challenged them as status-quo oriented, and it has been asserted that such thinking contributed to the American policy in Vietnam. This criticism is essentially unfair. Not only is there no evidence that social scientific thinking *per se* had any direct impact upon Vietnam policy, but scientific international relations is an enormously wide blanket that covers wholly divergent outlooks; among its practitioners have been supporters of U.S. foreign policy such as Herman Kahn and Morton Kaplan, and opponents such as Anatol Rapoport, J. David Singer, and Kenneth Boulding. A more appropriate assessment of the implications of a

---

[5] E.g., see Klaus Knorr and Sidney Verba, eds., *The International System: Theoretical Essays* (Princeton, N.J.: Princeton University Press, 1961), pp. 2–3.

systematic understanding of international relations would involve a recognition that we are dealing with something that, like an airplane, a computer, or the ability to speak a foreign language, can be put to totally different uses depending upon the inclination of its wielder. New techniques offer at least as much—and possibly more —potential use to the critics of America's foreign policy as to its supporters; particularly inasmuch as the existence of reliable knowledge contributes to the effectiveness of reasoned criticism, which is one of the tools available in seeking to bring about governmental policy changes, whether from within or from without. At any rate, the present state of the discipline is insufficiently advanced to permit significant instrumental application of it to advance the purposes of any group of power wielders. So the uses of scientific international relations theory are mainly in offering understanding or insights to the student, scholar, or practitioner of international affairs.

As a test of the validity or usefulness of any theory, there are three major demands we can make of it. The first of these requirements is *description*. Depending on the level of abstraction, the theory must accurately depict or represent the events that take place in the real world; and in fact most theories do provide description of some kind. Yet accurate description of a very complex reality seldom is possible without a certain measure of distortion. Because description involves selection, and therefore explanatory theory of at least a rudimentary sort, it leads us to the second requirement, *explanation*. Many theories offer explanations of why events take place, but the nature, accuracy, and rationality of these explanations vary enormously. Thus, for example, the occurrence of conflict may be ascribed to accident, human wickedness or folly, various types of imperialism, an international communist conspiracy, or a rigidifying of the balance of power. Explanation must say something about the causes of events, and statements about causes imply a predictive hypothesis, so a theory of international relations may be required to meet the test of *prediction*.[6] If this were understood in terms of a

---

[6] However, it is possible to predict without being able to understand. For further discussion of the relation between explanation and prediction, see Abraham Kaplan, *The Conduct of Inquiry* (San Francisco: Chandler, 1964), pp. 349–50. J. David Singer finds explanation to be the primary purpose of theory and also to be far more demanding than certain kinds of prediction. For his lucid treatment of the relationships between description, explanation, and prediction, see "The Level-of-Analysis Problem in International Relations," in Knorr and Verba, *The International System*, pp. 77–92; also reprinted in

requirement to predict specific events, it would create a virtually insurmountable problem. However, if prediction is interpreted more loosely, to deal with patterns of outcomes or with a general outcome rather than the specific pathway to that outcome, the chances of successful prediction are more favorable. For example, based on available statistics it would be possible to cite an entering class of 1,000 students at a university and predict that within three years a specific percentage of them would have gotten married. Although it would be impossible to predict with certainty when and where a given student might meet his prospective spouse (e.g., at a political demonstration in his second year or at a formal dinner in his third), the broader prediction would in fact hold true. Aggregate human phenomena, no matter how diverse, unpredictable and free-willed the behavior of individuals may be, display observable regularities; and insurance companies, mortgage firms and the manufacturers of bridal gowns make a great deal of money based on social prediction. Morton Kaplan has admitted that his theory of the international system could not have predicted the Hungarian Revolution of 1956; but he asks why require this of theory. Karl Deutsch has noted that by the criteria of Gross National Product, population, resources and arms production, it could have been predicted that the Americans had a very high probability of defeating the Japanese in World War II, but that any one specific sequence out of a multitude of possible pathways to this outcome was not readily predictable. The lesson of this example is that the significant prediction concerned the question of ultimate victory or defeat rather than the winning or losing of specific battles.

Seen in this light, one of the major traditional arguments against the possibility of laws in the study of human behavior loses force. According to this argument, based on the historical importance of the trigger mechanism, the smallest causes may produce the greatest effects in human affairs so the application of scientific method is regarded as "out of the question." [7] Pascal expressed an early version of this objection when he asserted that had Cleopatra's nose been a quarter-inch longer, the history of the world would have been

---

James N. Rosenau, ed., *International Politics and Foreign Policy* (New York: The Free Press, and London: Collier-Macmillan Ltd., rev. ed., 1969), pp. 20–29.

[7] W.S. Jevons, *The Principles of Science* (London, 1892), p. 761, quoted in Abraham Kaplan, *The Conduct of Inquiry*, p. 119.

different. But a leading philosopher of social science counters by observing that merely because not all events follow a foreseeable pattern does not mean that none do. "The fact is that in numberless instances every day we can and do recognize patterns in human behavior." [8] Without this ability we could not begin to cope with human affairs, let alone understand and theorize about them. In sum, while predictions of individual or micro-level phenomena may be difficult, broader or macro-level predictions can be made with substantial reliability, and it is the latter category that often bears the greater significance.

Still another argument holds that because each person is unique, and laws deal with what is common to many instances, scientific laws of human behavior cannot be formulated at all. But although, in a sense, every individual case is unique, laws in any science group individual items only on the basis of similarity in some respects, not on the basis of identity. As Abraham Kaplan puts it:

uniqueness does not imply nothing is shared but only that not everything is common to them. . . . A law requires repeatability . . . but what recurs is not one and the same instance—for this kind of recurrence is contradictory—but another instance sufficiently like the former ones to serve the purposes of the generalization of which it is an instance. And this requirement applies to laws about human beings as to laws about anything else.[9]

b) Individual freedom is not incompatible with natural law. Freely made choices can still exhibit statistical regularities, as for example in the case of suicide, where the individual events "triggering" a suicide are not identifiable in particular cases, but many factors of real statistical significance have nonetheless been identified.[10]

c) There remains another dimension that involves prediction and the application of theories. This is the tradeoff between precision and generality. The more precise one seeks to make a theory, the more variables need to be considered and therefore the more complicated it becomes. Specificity of treatment is thus obtained at the cost of generality and the power to analyze broad patterns of events. Theory itself is constructed by making simplifying assumptions

---

[8] A. Kaplan, *The Conduct of Inquiry*, p. 119.
[9] Ibid., p. 9.
[10] Ibid., pp. 120–21.

about reality, yet the more one seeks to apply theory, the more one is faced with the need to reexamine the basic abstractions that underlie it.[11] Thus overarching theory, which might offer a unified conception for making sense of international relations, is particularly difficult. More promising are partial theories and also techniques of analysis that apply to specific areas of international behavior.

At this point, having already treated some key aspects of "theory," it becomes appropriate to consider more precisely what the term actually means. At its loosest, theory may be a designation for almost any kind of orientation, conceptual framework, or even technique of analysis. But sharp distinctions must be made between these separate uses. Anatol Rapoport has called attention to four distinct meanings of theory, and his treatment of the subject provides a particularly apt means of classification. There is, first, the rigorous and specialized meaning of theory as used in the natural sciences, where theory "is a collection of derived theorems tested in the process of predicting events from observed conditions." [12] These theorems must be translatable into assertions about the real world, and some of them need to be verifiable. Such a use of theory can be made by the natural sciences because problems of recognition, definition, and classification have largely been solved. For the social sciences, however, these problems are often critical, hence the aim of the social sciences must be "lower" than that of the natural sciences. This second meaning of theory covers an activity that "aims only at subjective understanding," and that implies an "intuitive organization of perception." [13] This in turn leads Rapoport to identify a third meaning of theory, which inheres in the attempt of social science to gain intuitive understanding of social behavior, institutions, political systems, and cultures. "To 'support' a theory in this context means at

---

11 Knorr and Verba, *The International System*, pp. 2–3. For criticism of the tendency of observers to shift their focus carelessly between systemic and national levels, see Singer, "The Level-of-Analysis Problem," in Rosenau, *International Politics and Foreign Policy*, pp. 21 ff. The implications of studies at these different levels are also treated by Richard N. Rosecrance, *Action and Reaction in World Politics* (Boston: Little, Brown, 1963), chapter 1.

12 Anatol Rapoport, "Various Meanings of 'Theory'," *American Political Science Review* 52 (December, 1958): 980. This first meaning is also akin to the "strict" definition of theory set out by Morton Kaplan, which he subsequently relaxes. See below, chapter 6, p. 136.

13 Rapoport, "Various Meanings of 'Theory'," p. 981.

best to marshal factual material (historical and political events, case histories, etc.) in such a way that the reader who views this 'evidence' through the metaphors, concepts and definitions of which the 'theory' is constructed will have the experience of 'understanding'." [14] Finally, there is a fourth use of theory, in a normative sense, that applies to what is usually considered to be "political theory," and that typically deals with what "ought" to be. Yet even at such a distance from the physical sciences, there is still a possible relationship to science. Rapoport points out that Galileo described not how bodies actually fall but how they ought to fall under idealized conditions. Hence there is a sense in which normative theory can still be scientific. These meanings of theory become progressively less scientific, but Rapoport cautions that the value of a theory is not determined by any rigid criteria. Thus analogies and metaphors, while not providing scientific explanation, may be important in laying the groundwork for more precise investigations. "It is in this sense that the so-called 'models' of the non-exact sciences are to be appreciated." [15]

The meaning of theory is not only a question of whether it is more or less scientific. Theory can also be classified according to several other criteria. Stanley Hoffmann has suggested that we heed the degree of elaboration of a theory: whether it simply presents methodological questions, or at a more complex stage offers hypotheses to guide research, or ultimately provides explanatory laws. There is also the matter of scope: in any of these categories, efforts may be made to develop theories that are either partial or general. Indeed, theories may vary by object: empirical, philosophical, or policy-oriented.[16]

Finally, theory may not only be considered by the degree of its scientific orientation and extent of its elaboration, scope and objective, but also by its usefulness. In this sense a good theory will provide a means for organizing and classifying data. Without a theoretical model, all facts are likely to seem equally relevant.[17] A theory may therefore be judged on how well it provides criteria of selection

---

[14] Ibid., p. 982.

[15] Ibid.

[16] Stanley H. Hoffmann, *The State of War: Essays on the Theory and Practice of International Politics* (New York and London: Praeger, 1965), pp. 5–6.

[17] Thomas S. Kuhn, *The Structure of Scientific Revolutions* (Chicago: University of Chicago Press, 1962), p. 15.

and classification, and implicitly by its usefulness in guiding research, as well as by its accuracy and power in description, explanation, and prediction.

III. Is Scientific International Relations Theory Possible?

In recent years a debate has raged over the feasibility of a scientific approach to the study of international relations. While questions of scope and method are of real importance, the controversy has consumed a disproportionate share of the time and attention of international relations scholars. Indeed, nearly as much attention may have been devoted to how to study international relations as to the subject matter itself; and the debate is only gradually abating. Therefore it will here suffice to do no more than trace the broad outlines of the controversy in order to provide a background for those not already familiar with the major arguments.

Numerous approaches and subtleties exist, but there are basically two contending orientations, the traditional, or classical, and the scientific, or behavioral.[18] The essence of the traditionalist argument is that politics involves purpose in a way physical science does not; that scientific knowledge applies to matters of fact, but for areas involving human purpose, wisdom and intuition are necessary; that science requires a degree of precision and measurement that makes it unable to deal with the main elements of international politics; and that those undertaking the scientific approach can never be certain that they have not omitted something from their model.[19] In another formulation, a leading traditionalist argues that the scientific approach is even harmful to the extent that it may ultimately displace the classical approach. According to Hedley Bull, the practitioners of science, by confining themselves to what can only be verified according to strict procedures, deny themselves the only

---

[18] See, for example, Hedley Bull, "International Theory: The Case for a Classical Approach," *World Politics* 18 (April, 1966): 363–77; and Morton Kaplan, "The New Great Debate: Traditionalism versus Science in International Relations," *World Politics* 19 (October, 1966): 1–20.
[19] M. Kaplan, "The New Great Debate," p. 1.

tools presently available for coming to grips with the substance of international relations. Their forswearing of intuitive guesses "keeps them (or would keep them if they really adhered to it) as remote from the substance of international politics as the inmates of a Victorian nunnery were from the study of sex."[20] Scientific international relations is thus said to be without the means of coming to grips with such moral and empirical questions as what the place of war is, whether force is ever just, whether and when outside intervention in the internal affairs of a state is ever right, and to what extent international events may be determined by an international system. Bull argues that scientific international relations necessarily shies away from such questions and instead devotes itself to peripheral subjects such as methodology and logical extrapolations of conceptual frameworks. He says that whenever practitioners of the scientific approach have actually cast light on international relations it has been by resort to classical method; they are likely to remain in constant debate over fundamentals, their models are dangerous simplifications whose tidiness lends a specious air of authority, their work is impoverished by a fetish for measurement, and by cutting themselves off from history and philosophy they develop a view of the subject that is "callow and brash." Bull concludes by arguing that the contributions of scientific international relations, particularly its rigor and precision, can be readily accommodated within the classical approach. According to Bull, the proponents of science see themselves as "tough-minded and expert new men, taking over an effete and woolly discipline," [21] but their distinctive methods and approaches are leading them down a false path. "To all appeals to follow them down it we should remain resolutely deaf." [22]

By contrast, a leading proponent of the scientific approach replies that the traditionalists fail to understand the scientific assertions and techniques. They are said to confuse the methodological issues, to wrongly accuse science of using deterministic models despite explicit statements to the contrary, to mistake statements about models for statements about the real world, to carelessly lump together scientific approaches that have little in common, and to call for historical research without realizing that they fail to heed their

---

[20] Bull, "International Theory," p. 366.
[21] Ibid., p. 362.
[22] Ibid., p. 377.

own call and that they merely repeat the words of the scientific advocates. Finally, their criticisms are dismissed as "gross mistakes" and "ill-informed." [23]

Can we then hope to theorize about international relations in a way that can justifiably be called scientific? Certainly the subject matter is formidable in its difficulty. Albert Einstein was once asked, "Why is it that when the mind of man has stretched so far as to discover the structure of the atom we have been unable to devise the political means to keep the atom from destroying us?" He replied, "That is simple, my friend, it is because politics is more difficult than physics." [24] But the obvious difficulty of the subject does not signify that scientific treatment of it is impossible. After all, man at one time believed that electricity could not be measured nor the atom split, and the recent moon landings would have seemed not long ago to be sheer fantasy. While evidence of progress in natural science does not prove that there will be such advances in social science, its record at least implies that there is no reason to allow the complexity of the subject matter to deter efforts at progress.

It is true that perfect prediction is unattainable; we shall probably never be able to predict the Lee Harvey Oswalds or Sirhan Sirhans. But as terribly important as individual random events may be, we need to seek the observed regularities of human behavior; that is, to make predictions that are valid for the collectivity even if not for the individual. More importantly, it is not widely recognized that even physical science is not itself 100 percent precise.[25] Its modes of thought are actually probabilistic, and causality is treated as a special case of probability that only approaches, but does not reach 1.0. In other words, scientists speak of laws even though the actual relationships occur less than 100 percent of the time. This view of science contrasts markedly with that of Newtonian physics, which prevailed from the late 17th to the late 19th century and which described a universe in which everything happened precisely according to rigid laws. By implication such a universe would make scientific international relations, or indeed any social science, im-

---

[23] M. Kaplan, "The New Great Debate," p. 20.
[24] Quoted in John N. Herz, *International Politics in the Atomic Age* (New York: Columbia University Press, 1962), p. 214n.
[25] The following discussion is based on Norbert Wiener, *The Human Use of Human Beings* (London: Sphere, 1968; first published 1950), pp. 11–14.

possible because it would require an unattainable level of precision. But around the turn of the century Willard Gibbs (in America) and Ludwig Bolzmann (in Germany) applied statistics to physics and developed profoundly new ideas. Gibbs proposed a scientific method for taking into consideration uncertainty and contingency. Because no physical measurements can ever be utterly precise, Gibbs argued the necessity for introducing the element of chance into physics. The essence of this approach was revolutionary in that physics no longer claimed to deal with what would always happen but rather with what would happen with an overwhelming probability. Norbert Wiener, who utilized Gibbs' insights in developing the ideas of cybernetics, observed that "this recognition of an element of incomplete determinism, almost an irrationality in the world, is in a certain way parallel to Freud's admission of a deep irrational component in human conduct and thought." [26]

The point of this discussion is that Gibbs' conception of physics opens the theoretical possibility of scientific procedures in the social sciences, including international relations. For if physical science deals with uncertainties, then the difference between it and social science is not insurmountably qualitative but quantitative, and therefore not unbreachable. It may be true that "the search for an inclusive, water-tight definition of science which would apply to all fields of study is a waste of time," [27] but the problem is mainly one of semantics. What really matters is that basic scientific *procedures* are not totally beyond our reach.

Scientific procedures in the social sciences are thus possible and the commitment to a scientific orientation has been the *raison d'être* of the behavioral approach. This movement grew out of a dissatisfaction with the historical, institutional and philosophical approaches that characterized conventional political science.[28] Although divergent views exist among those characterized as "behavioralists," it is possible to describe a number of shared characteristics. Behavioralists view political science and international relations as social sciences, hence they are attuned to the borrowing of insights and even theories from such disciplines as economics,

---

[26] Ibid., p. 14.
[27] H. Victor Wiseman, *Politics: The Master Science* (London: Routledge & Kegan Paul, 1969), p. 39.
[28] See Robert A. Dahl, "The Behavioral Approach in Political Science: Epitaph for a Monument to a Successful Protest," *American Political Science Review* 55 (December, 1961): 763–72.

psychology, sociology, and anthropology. They seek to explain political events scientifically, and in their view science is both a way of organizing information and a set of directives on how to go about acquiring new knowledge.[29] Science implies a quest for similarities that is expressed in explicit and replicable procedures of classification and deduction. In this sense science designates a way of regulating information, discovering and validating new knowledge, and coordinating these undertakings in a collective endeavor.[30] As one of the most lucid of the behavioral scholars of international relations notes, "Science is not a substitute for insight, and methodological rigor is not a substitute for wisdom. Research which is *merely* rigorous may well be routine, mechanical, trivial, and of little theoretical or policy value. However . . . in the absence of such rigorous and controlled analysis even the most operational data are of little value." [31]

If scientific procedures in the study of international relations are theoretically possible, it is also worth examining just how its practitioners have sought to apply them. A wide variety of criteria exist, but one useful list establishes three tests of behavioralism.[32] The first test is that of uniformity. A study must be based on the assumption of discoverable behavioral regularities in the relationships being investigated. The second is precision. The study must be concerned with precise description and measurement. This often—though by no means always—means quantification. The third criterion is that of testable propositions. The conclusions of the study must include propositions that can be tested or verified by methods that are replicable by other investigators. However, in at least one area, recent work that meets these behavioral criteria has had certain

[29] Nelson W. Polsby, Robert A. Dentler, and Paul A. Smith, "A Brief Introduction to the Scientific Study of Political Behavior," in Polsby, Dentler and Smith, eds., *Politics and Social Life,* p. 4.

[30] Ibid., pp. 7–8.

[31] J. David Singer, "The Behavioral Science Approach to International Relations: Payoff and Prospects," *SAIS Review,* 10 (Summer, 1966): 12–20, reprinted in Rosenau, ed., *International Politics and Foreign Policy,* pp. 65–69. The quotation occurs on p. 67.

[32] Robert E. Riggs, et al., "Behavioralism in the Study of the United Nations," *World Politics* 22 (January, 1970): 201. Riggs also sets out the criteria of J. David Singer and David Easton.

limitations. Thus in studies of the United Nations, the approach has been no guarantee against "triviality, banality, or fuzzy-mindedness."[33] Technique has been exalted over substance, unwarranted assumptions have been made about statistical indicators and the underlying variables they are supposed to represent, intuitive judgments are inadequately distinguished from demonstrated propositions, and development of the work has not been cumulative. What is more, this research has been "most disappointing in the area of its central concern, that of theory-building," and no coherent theoretical system is expected to emerge in the foreseeable future.[34] More broadly, there is also a problem of fashionableness in the use of certain methods and techniques. Abraham Kaplan identifies the *law of the instrument*: "Give a small boy a hammer, and he will find that everything he encounters needs pounding."[35] Hence methods may be adopted regardless of their appropriateness for a given study. It has been noted that the contributors to a recent leading work on quantitative international relations reported approximately 1,600 correlation coefficients, though these often provide inadequate or misleading statistical measurement, and not a single use of the sometimes more appropriate regression coefficient.[36]

To sum up, scientific international relations is theoretically possible, but the difficulty comes in discovering and formulating the observable regularities of human behavior. While shortcomings exist in some of the work so far undertaken, the continuation of this enterprise may well be potentially quite fruitful. At a minimum, the behavioral approach, when undertaken from an existing basis of solid understanding, including historical and philosophical dimensions, as well as a sense of *mesure*, offers possibilities in understanding and in the generation of new insights and ideas that the classical approach may not include.

---

[33] Ibid., p. 230.

[34] Ibid., pp. 230–31. Riggs does argue that the behavioral approach has promoted better understanding of international organization, through its search for behavioral uniformities, and that it is also producing a body of low level theory with a solid base.

[35] A. Kaplan, *The Conduct of Inquiry*, p. 28.

[36] Edward R. Tufte, "Improving Data Analysis in Political Science," *World Politics* 21 (July, 1969): 642, 646. The reference concerns J. David Singer, ed., *Quantitative International Politics* (New York: Free Press, 1968).

IV. Some Contemporary
Approaches and Theories

It is not the purpose of this book to set forth an elaborate and all-encompassing view of international reality, nor even to present a comprehensive treatment of contemporary approaches and theories on the subject. What follows, in the succeeding chapters of this work, is a choice of areas based upon the judgment of potential fruitfulness or heuristic value, and—inevitably—upon the author's own interests. Although the array of topics thus omits a number of important theoretical areas (decision making, bureaucratic politics, linkage politics, strategic theory), it nonetheless includes a divergent enough range so as to illuminate the possibilities and limitations of contemporary systematic theorizing in international relations. Thus chapter two, Game Theory, discusses the uses of "Chicken" and "Prisoner's Dilemma" as models of war and peace and in application to the Soviet-American arms race and the Cuban Missile Crisis. The chapter also treats the conditions under which such games may help (or mislead) us in appreciating the dynamics of international politics. Chapter three, Integration Theory, deals with the area in which international relations theory is, in certain respects, most advanced. It offers a consideration of federalism, functionalism, and communications theory as approaches to regional integration; it treats the possibilities of measuring integration; and it then discusses some of the theoretical strengths and weaknesses in the field. Chapter four deals with Cybernetics and Communications Theory. After setting out the nature of cybernetic theory and of communications processes in machines, men, and institutions, it explores the use of transaction flow indices and other cybernetic techniques as sometimes-powerful tools of analysis. Next, chapter five provides a more systematic orientation to the perennial problems of power and conflict. This chapter contrasts traditional views with contemporary insights, and it treats the Middle East situation as a case of system-generated conflict. Chapter six deals with Systems Theory, the broadest, most ambitious—and sometimes the most opaque—of the approaches treated in this volume, and it gives particular attention to its present shortcomings. Finally, chapter seven is concerned with the ultimate possibilities of theory. It contrasts the place of tradition versus that of science, and sets out the necessary relationship between theory, public policy, and political values.

BIBLIOGRAPHY

BURTON, JOHN. *International Relations: A General Theory.* London and New York: Cambridge University Press, 1965.

DEUTSCH, KARL W. *The Analysis of International Relations.* Englewood Cliffs, N.J.: Prentice-Hall, 1968. The best single introductory work on the subject. Thought-provoking and highly readable.

EULAU, HEINZ. *The Behavioral Persuasion in Politics.* New York: Random House, 1963. An essay on the behavioral approach to the study of politics.

HOFFMANN, STANLEY. *Contemporary Theory in International Relations.* Englewood Cliffs, N.J.: Prentice-Hall, 1960. A useful collection of readings, together with Hoffmann's interpretive discussion.

KAPLAN, ABRAHAM. *The Conduct of Inquiry.* San Francisco: Chandler, 1964. A well-written and comprehensive treatment of behavioral science methodology.

KAPLAN, MORTON, ed. *New Approaches to International Relations.* New York: St. Martin's Press, 1968. A symposium of some important and sophisticated behavioral work. See especially Kaplan's introductory essay. Not easy reading.

KNORR, KLAUS, and ROSENAU, JAMES, eds. *Contending Approaches to International Politics.* Princeton, N.J.: Princeton University Press, 1969. A very literate and readable collection of essays. The Singer contribution is outstanding.

KUHN, THOMAS S. *The Structure of Scientific Revolutions.* Chicago: University of Chicago Press, 1962.

MCCLELLAND, CHARLES. *Theory and the International System.* New York: Macmillan, 1966.

ROSECRANCE, RICHARD N. *Action and Reaction in World Politics: International Systems in Perspective.* Boston: Little, Brown, 1963. Views history as the greatest data source for the social sciences. A "systematic empirical analysis."

ROSENAU, JAMES, ed. *International Politics and Foreign Policy.* rev. ed. New York: Free Press, 1969. A massive reference work containing a useful selection of the major approaches.

WISEMAN, H. VICTOR. *Politics: The Master Science.* London: Routledge & Kegan Paul, 1969. An examination of the place of science in the study of politics by a late, distinguished, British scholar.

2

Game

Theory

I. Introduction: What Is
Game Theory?

Game theory is a special kind of analysis of bargaining and conflict. Its essential elements can be found in such diverse situations as poker, chess, negotiations over the purchase of a house, or confrontation with a crying baby. But game theory is particularly applicable to politics, especially to the study of decision making, diplomacy, strategic deterrence and warfare.

The significance of game theory is that it allows us to analyze social situations while taking into account the existence of conflict as an often inevitable accompaniment rather than as an evil that must be eliminated. It also offers a means of dealing with decision making in which one side has incomplete control of the final outcome because of the presence of other independent decision-makers.

Game theory provides a number of advantages for the analysis of international relations. It requires that a conflict situation or decision process be examined from the point of view of the utilities and disadvantages that alternative courses of action offer to each participant. Since it postulates a setting in which both sides make rational calculations of their own self-interest, game theory offers the opportunity of viewing one's antagonist as something other than an incompetent swine or omniscient superman. Because game theory can offer the opportunity for quantitative procedures and for the systematic treatment and comparison of otherwise diverse situations, advocates of game theory have tended to argue that if a problem is genuinely understood it can also be represented by a mathematical model.[1] But its opponents have countered by saying that such reduction of a problem results in oversimplification and sterility. There are elements of truth in both arguments. While, in principle, any verbal expression can be reduced to a mathematical model, the precision and analytic power of the mathematical model are often obtained by a narrowing of focus and by the omission of complex qualifying statements. But a good model nonetheless enables us to pursue a line of reasoning that would otherwise be difficult or impossible to follow.[2]

To understand the operation of game theory it is first necessary to grasp some relatively straightforward definitions and assumptions. A basic assumption made by game theory involves a special kind of rationality, borrowed in its essentials from economics. One such definition is offered by Anthony Downs:

A rational man is one who behaves as follows: (1) he can always make a decision when confronted with a range of alternatives; (2) he ranks all the alternatives facing him in his order of preference in such a way that each is either preferred to, indifferent to, or inferior to each other; (3) his preference ranking is transitive; (4) he always chooses from among the possible alternatives that which ranks highest in his preference ordering; and (5) he always makes the same decision each time he is confronted with the same alternatives.[3] – assumes other things equal.

In other words, each side in the game has consistent and transitive preferences. The decision-makers, or *players*, may be persons, social groups of any kind, or countries. In any given game, the players usually have divergent goals and face two or more possible outcomes to which they assign different values, or *payoffs*. Each player seeks to maximize his own payoffs while keeping in mind the fact that he must act in the presence of other players with conflicting or at least divergent interests, whose choices will partially determine

---

[1] Martin Shubik treats this in *Game Theory and Related Approaches to Social Behavior* (New York: John Wiley & Sons, 1964), p. 3.
[2] Ibid.
[3] Anthony Downs, *An Economic Theory of Democracy* (New York: Harper & Row, 1957), p. 6. Downs has abstracted conditions from chapters 1 and 2 of Kenneth J. Arrow, *Social Choice and Individual Values* (New York: Wiley, 1951).

the outcome and payoff of the game. Commonly, the alternative choices, possible outcomes and payoffs are displayed in a chart called a *payoff matrix*. In their essentials, as set out by Anatol Rapoport, all games share the following features: first, there must be two or more players; second, the game begins by one or more of the players choosing between a number of specific alternatives; third, after the initial choice is made, a certain situation results that partly determines the alternatives open to the next player, as well as who is to make the next choice; fourth, the choices made by the players may or may not become known (games in which they are known are termed "games of perfect information," e.g., chess); fifth, if a game involves successive choices, there is a "termination rule" (e.g., "checkmate" in chess); and sixth, every game ends in a certain situation.[4] If the application of these rules seems less than obvious, their relevance will be more evident when we consider some specific examples.

II. The Two-Person
Zero-Sum Game

The simplest type of game is called the two-person zero-sum game. This means that there are only two players, and that whatever one gains is precisely what the other loses. Gains and losses cancel each other out, or add to zero, hence the term *zero-sum*. This type of game is one of pure opposition; it can be found in most card games, chess, duels, and some kinds of warfare. While the two-person zero-sum game offers some intriguing examples, political life does not display a great many situations of this sort, hence certain complicating elements are added to the basic model in order to bring it closer to the kinds of political questions with which we are concerned. The first major alteration to the basic two-person zero-sum game is to add extra players. This makes it an *n-person zero-sum game*. Examples of this would be a multi-handed poker game or a duel involving three or more persons. In practice, the calculations and payoff matrices of n-person games quickly become exceedingly complex, although they retain the limitations of zero-sum games; for this reason many of

---

[4] Anatol Rapoport, *Two-Person Game Theory* (Ann Arbor: University of Michigan Press, 1969), pp. 18–20.

the more fruitful game theory examples are restricted to two-person games. A more rewarding basic alteration, and one that moves game theory closer to political reality, involves the non-zero sum, or *variable-sum game*. This type of game involves payoff matrices that do not necessarily provide that the amount of one player's gain is exactly equal to the other's loss. Instead, there are situations in which both players may gain, both may lose, or they may win or lose varying amounts. The variable-sum game is said to introduce the idea of nature, or of a bank. The players may be thought of as being in cooperation to maximize the sum of their payoffs but in conflict over how to distribute it.[5] Thus they may even have shared interests, as in the case of the United States and USSR finding it to their mutual benefit to avoid nuclear war.

Because games can be either two-person or n-person, zero-sum or variable-sum, there are four possible types of games (Figure 2-1).

FIGURE 2-1

Four Different Types of Games

Type of Payoffs

	zero-sum	variable-sum
2-person	2-person zero-sum (e.g., chess, 2-hand poker, some kinds of warfare)	2-person variable sum (e.g., U.S.–USSR arms race; also "Chicken" and "Prisoner's Dilemma")
n-person	n-person zero-sum (e.g., multi-handed poker, 3-person duel)	n-person variable sum (e.g., U.S.–USSR–China arms race)

Number of persons

---

[5] W. J. M. MacKenzie, *Politics and Social Science* (Harmondsworth, Middlesex: Pelican, Penguin Books, 1967), p. 128.

A mathematical formula for the n-person variable-sum game is the ideal model, but it is unavailable because of its complexity. Thus we will here concentrate upon the more manageable, and not entirely unrealistic, two-person variable-sum games of which "Chicken" and "Prisoner's Dilemma" offer the most intriguing possibilities for stimulating thought about problems of international relations.

III. "Chicken" and "Prisoner's Dilemma" as Models of War and Peace

The well-known game of "Chicken" has several variations but the basic elements of each are nearly identical. One such version involves two teenagers driving stolen cars. In the presence of their contemporaries they line up at opposite ends of a stretch of roadway, then drive at full speed directly toward one another. Each driver has two choices: to swerve or not to swerve, but whoever swerves first is "chicken." There are thus four possible outcomes for this game. If the two drivers, here designated as player A and player B, swerve simultaneously, both are "chicken" but neither loses face. If A swerves and B does not, then A is "chicken" and B gains status among his peers. Alternatively, if B swerves and A does not, the payoffs are reversed. Finally, if both continue straight ahead without swerving, they crash; the payoff in this case is death.

This slightly macabre game has in fact certain analogies with international confrontations. The relationship can be more clearly illustrated if we display a payoff matrix for Chicken (Figure 2-2). Each player has two alternatives. He may swerve, a course of action that we will designate "a_1" for A, and "b_1" for B, or he may refuse to swerve, which we will label as "a_2" for A, and "b_2" for B. Each box, or *cell*, in the payoff matrix represents one of the four possible outcomes. The payoff to A is shown in the lower left-hand corner of each cell, the payoff to B in the upper right. The numbers assigned to the various outcomes reflect the values, or *utilities*, that each of the "rational" players derives from the possible outcomes. Thus if both swerve (a course of action that is designated a_1b_1) they each neither gain nor lose and they each receive a payoff of zero. If A swerves and B does not (a_1b_2) then A receives a payoff of -10, reflecting his loss of face, and B's payoff is $+10$, reflecting his gain of status. If

FIGURE 2-2

Chicken

	B	
	b_1 *swerve*	b_2 *don't swerve*
a_1 *swerve*	0 a_1b_1 (both swerve) 0	+10 gain status a_1b_2 lose face −10
a_2 *don't swerve*	−10 lose face a_2b_1 gain status +10	−100 death a_2b_2 (crash) death −100

both fail to swerve (a_2b_2) then the payoff value of −100 is placed, somewhat arbitrarily, upon their deaths. The matrix also illustrates the manner in which each player has only incomplete control over the outcome. While a player's choice can prevent certain outcomes, it cannot determine the precise outcome of the game; this results only from the choices of both players.

In the game of Chicken each player has a *dominant* strategy, which in this case happens to be swerving; hence the outcome a_1b_1 (both swerve) is regarded as being the most probable. This is due to what is called the *minimax* strategy. The notion was put forward by John Von Neumann and Oskar Morgenstern, who wrote the basic work on game theory, *The Theory of Games and Economic Behavior*.[6] They argue that the rational approach for each player is to adopt a strategy that guarantees the best of the worst possible outcomes. In other words, they posit a damage-minimizing strategy in

[6] Von Neumann and Morgenstern, *The Theory of Games and Economic Behavior* (Princeton, N.J.: Princeton University Press, 1944).

the face of the assumption that the environment will threaten the worst possible harm. Thus rather than deciding on the basis of maximizing the opportunity for gains, a player is to choose the strategy that assures the least bad outcomes, or minimizes his losses.[7] In Chicken this means that A is expected to observe that the worst that can befall him should he choose to swerve is a payoff of -10, whereas should he choose not to swerve, the worst possible outcome is -100. Therefore A will choose to swerve. Player B makes the same kind of calculation and also chooses to swerve. The outcome a_1b_1 (both swerve) is dominant and the game tends toward a certain equilibrium, or *saddlepoint*.[8]

The relationship of Chicken to international relations is somewhat less than fanciful. The obvious analogy is with crisis confrontations between America and Russia. In this analogy, with the United States being substituted for A and the USSR for B, the decision to swerve could be thought of as stepping back from the brink of nuclear war, while refusing to swerve can mean pursuing a given policy with total resolution even at the risk of nuclear war (Figure 2-3). Perhaps the dominance of the swerving strategy within the game of Chicken offers an aid to understanding why a nuclear peace (or at least non-war) has been maintained between the two superpowers in the postwar period. It also illuminates the kind of logic that may have applied at the time of the 1962 Cuba crisis, when, after their "eyeball to eyeball" confrontation with the United States, the Soviets gave in, suffering a certain loss of face but avoiding nuclear war. Cell a_2b_1 in Figure 2-3 would be an appropriate representation of that particular outcome.

There are ramifications of the Chicken game that, when applied to the study (or practice) of international relations offer discomforting implications. In particular these include the techniques of *precommitment* and the accompanying uses of irrationality. Herman

---

[7] Shubik, *Game Theory*, pp. 17–18.

[8] According to Anatol Rapoport, a saddlepoint is determined "if it turns out that some outcome is at the same time the worst in its row and the best in its column." *Two-Person Game Theory*, p. 195. For the Chicken matrix in Figure 2-2 above, the Rapoport definition is worded to reflect the saddlepoint from the calculation of B's payoff. Since some types of matrices illustrate the payoffs only for one player, it would here be necessary to reverse the words "row" and "column" in Rapoport's definition in order to find the same saddlepoint from A's point of view. It should also be noted that in certain games there can be more than one saddlepoint; other games can lack a saddlepoint altogether.

FIGURE 2-3

The U.S. Versus the USSR as a Chicken Game

B

(USSR)

	b_1 *swerve* *(restraint)*	b_2 *don't swerve* *(total resolution)* made C
a_1 *swerve* *(restraint)*	0 a_1b_1 (mutual restraint) 0	+10 gain status a_1b_2 lose face −10
a_2 *don't* *swerve* *(total* *resolution)* invade V	−10 lose face a_2b_1 gain status +10	−100 death a_2b_2 (nuclear war) death −100

A
(U.S.)

Kahn, in *Thinking About the Unthinkable*,[9] has embroidered the Chicken game to provide for the adoption by one of the players of a course of preliminary action that would convince the other of his unshakable determination to refuse to swerve once the race begins. Since such advance refusal would be irrational, A actually seeks to convince B of his irrationality. Thus before climbing into his car he may swagger, boast, threaten and attempt to appear generally irate

---

[9] Kahn, *Thinking About the Unthinkable* (New York: Avon, 1966). On precommitment, also see Thomas C. Schelling, *The Strategy of Conflict* (New York: Oxford University Press, 1963).

and unreasonable. Furthermore he may give the impression of drunkenness, which he may underscore by throwing empty liquor bottles out the window of his vehicle. He may put on dark glasses to reduce his vision, despite the confrontation taking place in the dead of night, and lastly, once the cars are headed toward each other, he may detach the steering wheel and hurl it out the window, thus confirming his unalterable precommitment to an unswerving course. What the irrationality and accompanying techniques seek to accomplish is to convince B of A's absolute dedication to the strategy of refusing to swerve. If the precommitment is in fact genuine it leaves B with only two possible outcomes, both unsatisfactory, instead of four. If B swerves he loses face (-10), if he refuses to swerve he dies (-100). Thus B, as a rational player, will necessarily seek to minimize his losses by choosing to swerve. A's uncompromising stance, aided by his display of irrationality, will have produced a handy victory. Kahn has dealt at some length with the uses of irrationality (e.g., "Do as I say or I'll blow my brains out all over your new suit!"), and Thomas Schelling has argued that deterrence even depends on convincing the other side that one is irrational enough to use nuclear weapons at the risk of mutual suicide.

Applied to Soviet–American confrontations, the lesson of precommitment would seem to reward the side willing to go closest to the brink of nuclear war. Hence the comment attributed to one of the participants on the Executive Committee ("Excom") of the National Security Council at the peak of the Cuba crisis: "We're eyeball to eyeball and I think the other fellow just blinked." But at this point Chicken breaks down as a model of international conflict, at least in prescriptive terms. For what Chicken does is to prepare the player for only the single crisis confrontation.[10] The difficulty lies in the inescapable predicament that, unlike the teenagers, neither side can quit and go home to bed after one play of the game. Instead, world politics imposes a survival game, the object of which is not so much to win an isolated engagement as to survive in order to play again and again. Even if precommitment guaranteed a 90 percent chance of success on any given play, the problem of repeated encounters would quickly reduce the chances of survival.

---

[10] Karl Deutsch calls attention to this key limitation in *Nerves of Government* (New York: Free Press, 1966), pp. 69–70. The following line of argument on decreasing cumulative probabilities is also his.

Thus the chances of remaining alive after two encounters, each of which required a strategy offering a 90 percent chance of staying alive, would not be 90 percent but .90 multiplied by .90, or .81 (i.e., 81 percent). By the same logic, the chances for surviving through the seventh encounter would have fallen to less than half (.478). See Figure 2-4.

FIGURE 2-4

Individual Versus Cumulative Probabilities of Survival [11]

		Encounter						
		1	2	3	4	5	6	7
Probability of Survival	on the individual encounter	.9	.9	.9	.9	.9	.9	.9
	cumulative (after nth encounter)	.9	.81	.729	.656	.590	.531	.478

It might be argued that the chances for success in a single crisis confrontation are better than 90 percent: even then the chances of survival would still deteriorate, though less rapidly. But the probabilities are almost certainly far less reassuring than even the 90 percent figure would indicate. At the time of the Cuban missile crisis, no less a participant than President Kennedy reportedly estimated the probability of nuclear war as "somewhere between one out of three and even." [12] Repeated encounters involving probabilities of this order would mean an exceedingly high likelihood of disaster. To abstract the short-run lesson of the utility of precommitment and its accompanying techniques of irrationality from the game of

[11] Cumulative figures have been calculated as follows: assuming individual survival probability of .9, the probability of survival after the first encounter is .9. After the second encounter it is .9 × .9 = .81. After the third it is .81 × .9 = .729, etc.

[12] Theodore C. Sorenson, *Kennedy* (New York: Harper & Row, and London: Hodder and Stoughton, 1965), p. 705.

Chicken (and from the reality of the Cuba crisis) would greatly increase the probability of nuclear war in the not very long run.

There is another game that offers thought-provoking insights into the nature of international relations but that does not provide the possibly dangerous lessons of Chicken. *Prisoner's Dilemma* has been stated in a variety of forms and with differing numerical utilities, but it, too, is a game whose essentials remain similar throughout the various descriptions. In one popular interpretation two suspects are arrested and separated.[13] The public prosecutor is certain they are guilty of a specific crime but lacks evidence sufficient for conviction at a trial. He tells each prisoner that each has two alternatives: to confess to the crime the police are sure they have committed, or not to confess. *If both do not confess* then the prosecutor will book them on a minor trumped-up charge such as illegal possession of a weapon, and they will both get relatively minor punishment (one year in jail); *if both confess* they will be prosecuted, but he will recommend less than the most severe sentence (five years each); *if one confesses and the other does not* then the confessor will get lenient treatment for turning state's evidence (three months imprisonment) whereas the latter will suffer the maximum sentence (ten years). The elements of the game are represented in Figure 2-5.

Examining the matrix, we find that because each prisoner wants to maximize his own utilities, his rational strategy is to confess. The rational, or dominant, outcome is that both prisoners confess and both get five years. The "rational" outcome is not the best outcome; were they both to remain silent they both could spend only one year in jail instead of five. But player A calculates as follows: he does not know what B will do; if A chooses silence (a_1), the worst possible outcome would be ten years in jail (-100); if A chooses to confess (a_2), the worst possible outcome would be five years (-50). The minimax strategy thus dictates that he pick the least damaging of the worst possible outcomes, so he necessarily chooses to confess. A can also look at the situation another way: if he is silent his possible payoffs are one year (if B is silent) or ten years (if B confesses); if he confesses, his possible payoffs are three months (if B is silent)

---

[13] With a few alterations, this is basically the version presented by Robert D. Luce and Howard Raiffa in *Games and Decisions* (New York: Wiley, 1967), p. 95, italics added. But, see also Anatol Rapoport and Albert M. Chammah, *Prisoner's Dilemma: A Study in Conflict and Cooperation* (Ann Arbor: University of Michigan Press, 1965).

FIGURE 2-5

Prisoner's Dilemma

B

		b_1 silence	b_2 confess
A	a_1 silence	a_1b_1 (both silent) top: −10 / 1 year bottom: 1 year / −10	a_1b_2 top: −3 / 3 months bottom: 10 years / −100
	a_2 confess	a_2b_1 top: −100 / 10 years bottom: 3 months / −3	a_2b_2 (both confess) *saddle pt* top: −50 / 5 years bottom: 5 years / −50

or five years (if *B* confesses). Obviously, *A* prefers three months to one year, and five years to ten years, and since he has no communication with *B* nor control over *B*'s choice, he is better off to choose to confess regardless of what *B* does. Unfortunately for *A*, *B* makes the same calculations and also chooses to confess. The strategy of confession strictly dominates. The unique saddlepoint of the game is a_2b_2, mutual confession and five years in prison for each, despite the fact that had both remained silent, both would have spent only one year in jail.

The crucial lesson of Prisoner's Dilemma is that there are games in which the most rational competitive calculation for each side leads to harm for both, despite the existence of a different and mutually preferable alternative. The lesson is immensely revealing when applied to international relations because it can show us how a situation may lock two participants into conflict regardless of their individual wishes and even though both may be neither evil nor stupid. A model of the United States–USSR arms race (Figure 2-6) provides a good analogy. Here the United States faces virtually the same calculations as Player A in Prisoner's Dilemma. If the United States chooses low arms spending, the worst possible outcome for it is that the USSR will continue high arms spending and thus obtain a strong military and political advantage internationally, at a cost to the United States of −100 and a gain for the USSR of +50.[14] If the United States chooses high arms spending, the worst possible outcome is a mutually costly arms race (−50). By this calculation the United States would choose a strategy that offered the least harmful of two undesirable outcomes, and so would choose high arms spending. Looking at the situation another way, the United States comes to the same strategy: if it keeps arms expenditures low, its possible payoffs are arms control (if the USSR cooperates) or a serious disadvantage (if the USSR undertakes high arms spending); if the United States chooses high arms spending, its payoffs are a strong international advantage (if the USSR spends little) or an arms race (if the USSR spends much). The United States prefers an international advantage to arms control (+50 versus −10) and an arms race to international disadvantage (−50 versus −100), so the model implies that the United States is better off, regardless of what the USSR does, to choose high arms spending. Of course, according to the terms of the model, the USSR makes precisely the same calculations and it, too, chooses high arms spending. The dominant outcome is an arms race (a_2b_2). Each player spends vast sums yet derives no definite advantage over the other. Had both chosen to keep down their arms expenditures their relative equality would have been the same but they would have had vast resources to spend on other needs.

---

[14] The corresponding entries in the Prisoner's Dilemma matrix (Figure 2-5) were −100 (A's loss) and −3 (B's far smaller loss). However, assigning a utility for B of +50 seems more appropriate here given Soviet–American perceptions of the political and military importance of any serious advantage in the arms race. Both figures are arbitrary, but their relative significance in the two matrices is comparable. The rational choices and basic structure of the two games also remain comparable. However, under certain other numerical changes the nature of Prisoner's Dilemma can shift decisively. See Luce and Raiffa, *Games and Decisions*, pp. 94–101.

Figure 2-6

U.S.–USSR Arms Race as a Prisoner's Dilemma

		B (USSR)	
		b_1 *silence* *(low arms spending)*	b_2 *confess* *(high arms spending)*
a_1 *silence* *(low arms spending)*	A (U.S.)	−10 a_1b_1 (arms limitation) −10	+50 important USSR ad- vantage a_1b_2 serious U.S. disadvantage −100
a_2 *confess* *(high arms spending)*		−100 serious USSR disadvantage a_2b_1 important U.S. advantage +50	−50 a_2b_2 (arms race) −50

The same model could presumably be applied to arms races between other countries or to competitive development of individual
weapons systems such as the anti-ballistic missile (ABM). While
there are obvious simplifying assumptions about the model, it offers
considerable explanatory value in any analysis of the postwar United

States–USSR arms race. What the model does not do is say that the course of action followed was desirable or that it should continue. Instead it sheds light on the structural properties of a situation in which the two countries followed a course that was not to their mutual benefit but that had a grim rationality of its own.

Prisoner's Dilemma also possesses more complex implications. It has been set up as an experimental game, with players choosing alternative courses of action and receiving small monetary payoffs after each trial. The experimental results have shown that the ability of the players to communicate increases the tendency for coopera- tion.[15] Additionally, a learning process can take place, and more cooperation occurs if the players realize that the situation will be repeated indefinitely.[16] Since the superpowers do in fact com- municate, and since the experience of crisis confrontation (e.g., Cuba) does produce a certain learning effect, there is at least a possibility that the Prisoner's Dilemma relationship could experience an increased probability of more mutually beneficial choices in the future.

IV. Tacit Bargaining and Prominent Solutions

Another aspect of game theory that offers some aid to an understanding of international relations has to do with a type of communication known as *tacit bargaining*.[17] The value of this concept is to illustrate how communication can and does take place in situations of conflict where overt contact may not exist. It indicates that opposite sides may concert their intentions or expectations, even in the midst of war.

One type of tacit bargaining takes place in the presence of

---

15 Anatol Rapoport and C. Orwant, "Experimental Games: A Review," *Behavioral Science* 7 (January 1962): reprinted in Shubik, *Game Theory*, p. 296. Also Kellog V. Wilson and V. Edwin Bixenstine, "Forms of Social Control in Two-person Two-choice Games," *Behavioral Science* 7 (January 1962): re- printed in Shubik, *Game Theory*, p. 354. For a more detailed treatment of ex- perimental results, see Rapoport and Chammah, *Prisoner's Dilemma*, especially pp. 204–27.

16 Luce and Raiffa, *Games and Decisions*, pp. 100–101.

17 The ideas of tacit bargaining and prominent solutions are set out by Schelling, *The Strategy of Conflict*, Chapter 3.

divergent interests. Warfare offers prime examples. Thus processes of escalation and of limited war are said to involve "signalling" to an enemy. In World War II, despite unparalleled violence and suffering, neither side used poison gas. Presumably when one side refrained from doing so, this indicated a willingness to refrain as long as the other side did also. In another case, German treatment of Soviet prisoners of war was so brutal that the Russians reciprocated when the tide of battle later turned; but on the Western front the Germans tended to observe the Geneva Convention on the treatment of military prisoners of war and the Western allies followed the same practice. When such tacit agreements on limits are reached in the absence of communication, the parties must often rely on *prominent solutions*, or situations that somehow stand out from alternatives and are perceived as such by both sides.[18] Thus the present nuclear threshold possesses a critical importance despite the fact that nuclear explosives can be produced that are no more powerful than the largest conventional ones. The importance of the nuclear threshold is that the difference between conventional and nuclear is obvious and qualitative, while that between small and large nuclear weapons is only a matter of degree. Thus there is a recognizable limit that might obtain in the midst of warfare.

Thomas Schelling has offered some intriguing examples to illustrate the process of tacit bargaining. For example:

You and your partner (rival) are to be given $100 if you can agree on how to divide it without communicating. Each of you is to write the amount of his claim on a sheet of paper; and if the two claims add to no more than $100, each gets exactly what he claimed. If the two claims exceed $100, neither of you gets anything. How much do you claim? [19]

The obvious answer is $50, regardless of need, age or personal antagonism, and Schelling's informal sample produced 36 out of 40 respondents who chose this answer.

Tacit communication may also occur when the parties have shared, rather than divergent, interests. Here, in the absence of direct communication, those involved can often coordinate their actions or expectations with others if each is aware that the other

[18] Ibid., p. 75.
[19] Ibid., p. 61.

is trying to do the same. Schelling offers several additional problems as illustrations of this process. For example:

Name an amount of money. If you all name the same amount you can have as much as you named.[20]

In this case a plurality of Schelling's sample (12 of 41) chose $1 million, and only three persons chose numbers that were not a power of ten. The obvious reason for picking $1 million is that it is a prominent solution. Regardless of one's own preference, the answer is one that logically can be expected from most (American) players. Hence even if one hoped to get a greater sum of money, the prominence of the figure "one million" would be such as to lead to a consensus on that number in the absence of communication.

Just as in Chicken, however, there are pitfalls in seeking to extend the lessons too literally into international relations. The American policy of escalation in Vietnam, including bombing of the North, involved a process of signalling to the North Vietnamese. Unfortunately, the North Vietnamese and the Vietcong were willing to be "irrational." By their willingness to suffer casualties at a rate that the Americans would have regarded as unacceptable, they upset careful U.S. calculations. The resultant step-by-step escalation led only to stalemate at increasingly higher levels of cost to both sides.

V. Conclusion: The Value of Game Theory

How useful is game theory and how applicable to political life? Clearly, game theory rests on some very special assumptions. For example, the numbers in the payoff matrix reflect arbitrary calculations about certain values. To the extent that these figures are wisely arbitrary,[21] they can reflect useful information that the analyst or researcher knows on the basis of

---

[20] Ibid., pp. 55–56.

[21] An effective case for assigning numbers to ordered categories has been made by Edward Tuftee. He argues that "the researcher often knows more about the phenomenon than the mere ordering of observations implies; thus assigning numbers helps to build that additional information into measurement. . . . Of course it is arbitrary. The point . . . is to be *wisely* arbitrary." See "Improving Data Analysis in Political Science," *World Politics* 21 (July, 1969): 645.

careful investigation into the subject matter. Yet even if individual preferences were measurable, game theory assumes that these are fixed, that values among different decision-makers are comparable and ordered, that individuals possess reliable knowledge of various alternatives, and that they correctly perceive the value of certain outcomes and of the probabilities of attaining them.[22] All of these assumptions can be challenged; their justification would have to rest on the argument that they provide serviceable approximations of aggregate (rather than individual) behavior. There are additional problems: in real life, players may or may not move spontaneously, know how other players have moved, be beset by important time limitations, or possess incomplete, misleading or leaked information.[23] And before game theory can provide a truly reliable contribution to decision making, it must cope successfully with the n-person variable-sum game, for which no feasible matrix yet exists, but which reflects the nature of most international bargaining and conflict.

Apart from limits imposed by the special assumptions upon which game theory rests, there remains a problem in applying game theory to the full complexity of national government actions. A government is rarely a single player; instead it is a complex interplay of forces, some of which may convey their own signals or pursue their own strategies. Governments thus do not respond solely in reaction to external causes; their strategies are also influenced by purely internal and domestic factors. As a result, an American or Soviet government might, in the real world, choose a course of action that appears "irrational" in terms of game theory criteria.

Taking into account all these limitations, game theory still has considerable value. First, it offers a certain kind of rationality. By providing the opportunity to think seriously about situations in which one side has only partial control over the outcome, it helps to separate rational from ethical calculations. It offers an analysis of how, given special assumptions, people in conflict actually behave rather than how they ought to behave. Because it enables us to calculate how a conflict looks from the viewpoint of an antagonist, it forces us to make judgments about situations in which *both* sides make rational choices. Even if game theory merely contributed to rational thought about conflict (as opposed, for example, to thinking

---

[22] Shubik catalogues some of these objections, *Game Theory*, pp. 57–58.
[23] Ibid., pp. 17–19.

about one's antagonists as "inscrutable Orientals") this would be no small contribution. But game theory offers a second major advantage in suggesting important possibilities; in other words, it has considerable heuristic value. Like any sophisticated theory, game theory operates as a "generator of ideas." [24] While it cannot establish conclusions, it provides an invaluable stimulus to thought. Third, game theory provides insights into the nature and dynamics of international conflict. Thus Prisoner's Dilemma suggests why it is that regardless of the wishes or intelligence of individuals on opposite sides, an outcome harmful to their mutual interest may be likely. Perhaps by directing our attention to the structural properties of situations that may produce unintended and undesirable consequences, game theory carries us somewhat further in our understanding of conflict than does Bertrand Russell's attack—by no means entirely unjustified—on the wickedness and folly of statesmen. Lastly, because game theory may show us the existence of a myriad of assumptions, each leading to different choices and solutions, and because it thereby indicates that all problems do not necessarily have a "best choice" among various possible courses of action, one of the most serious and subtle thinkers on the subject has observed that "the great philosophical value of game theory is in its power to reveal its own incompleteness. Game theoretical analysis, if pursued to its own completion, perforce leads us to consider other than strategic modes of thought." [25]

BIBLIOGRAPHY

KAHN, HERMAN. *Thinking About the Unthinkable*. 2d ed. New York: Avon, 1966. A non-technical but controversial treatment of strategic thinking. Uses a number of game theory examples.

LUCE, R. DUNCAN and RAIFFA, HOWARD. *Games and Decisions*. New York: Wiley, 1967. An important technical work; accessible to the reader who has some mathematical background.

RAPOPORT, ANATOL. *Fights, Games and Debates*. Ann Arbor: University

---

[24] Rapoport, *Two-Person Game Theory*, p. 202. Similarly, Morton Kaplan describes his own use of game theory models as analytic and suggestive rather than rigorous and deductive.

[25] Rapoport, *Two-Person Game Theory*, p. 214.

of Michigan Press, 1960. A lucid introduction to the application of game theory in the social sciences.

————. *Strategy and Conscience*. New York: Schocken Books, 1969. A compelling treatment of the uses and abuses of game theory and strategic thinking.

————. *Two-Person Game Theory*. Ann Arbor: University of Michigan Press, 1969. Helpful presentation of the essential ideas. Written for the non-mathematician.

SCHELLING, THOMAS C. *The Strategy of Conflict*. New York: Oxford University Press, 1963. A path-breaking and highly readable work on the application of game theory, particularly to strategic questions.

SHUBIK, MARTIN, ed. *Game Theory and Related Approaches to Social Behavior*. New York: Wiley, 1964. Useful collection of articles. Includes an introductory essay on game theory by the author, and contains a comprehensive bibliography.

3

Integration

Theory

The development of integration theory has been heralded as one of the most significant advances in contemporary political science. It is said to provide great insights and to be truly comparative in its analyses.[1] This chapter will introduce some of the key ideas and applications of integration theory. After very briefly treating the federalist approach, it will turn to the two most important theories of integration: functionalism and the communications approach. The chapter will then consider the opportunities for measurement that these theories provide, and will conclude with an assessment of their possibilities and limitations as partial theories of international relations.

At its most basic, the concept of *integration* can be defined as forming parts into a whole or creating interdependence. Although several complex and somewhat divergent definitions of *political integration* exist, the concept basically denotes a relationship of community or strong cohesiveness among peoples in a political entity. It involves mutual ties and a sense of group identity and self-awareness.[2] There are two different levels at which integration can be considered. One is *national* and concerns the condition or process of integration within a single country. The other, with which we are mainly concerned here, is *regional* and applies to the development of integration between two or more separate countries. National integration can concern the success or failure of creating a

[1] Karl Kaiser, "The Interaction of Regional Subsystems: Some Preliminary Notes on Recurrent Patterns and the Role of Superpowers," *World Politics* 21 (October 1968): 86–89.

[2] Joseph S. Nye, "Comparative Regional Integration: Concept and Measurement," *International Organization* 21 (1968): 858. And Philip E. Jacob and Henry Teune, "The Integrative Process: Guidelines for Analysis of the Bases of Political Community," in Philip E. Jacob and James V. Toscano, eds., *The Integration of Political Communities* (Philadelphia: Lippincott, 1964), p. 4.

sense of nationhood within a recently independent entity such as Indonesia or Nigeria, or it can deal with more established states, such as Belgium or Canada, that have internal divisions involving language, religion, or ethnicity.[3] Regional integration typically involves groupings such as the European Economic Community or the East African Community.

I. Federalism

Federalism as a theory of regional integration has been roughly handled by most contemporary theorists. It combines description and prescription in asserting that the surest pathway to political community is by means of formal constitutional measures. Federalism regards the creation of federal institutions including military and police forces and a common legal system as the best method for uniting people who already share some common features such as language or culture or merely geographic proximity, but who live in separate states. (A federal arrangement is said to exist when a set of political communities are united in a common order, but retain their autonomy.) [4] Proponents of federalism expect that the establishment of common institutions will promote the growth of common attitudes and a sense of community. Hence they are preoccupied with written constitutions, different forms of representative institutions, and the division of powers between federal, national, and local levels. Most commonly, federalism is advocated as a means of bringing together previously separate entities to form a more effective or desirable common government.[5] By implication, federalism seeks to adapt institutions

---

[3] On national integration see, e.g., Reinhard Bendix, *Nation-Building and Citizenship* (New York: Wiley, 1964); Karl W. Deutsch and William J. Foltz, eds., *Nation-Building* (New York: Atherton, 1966); Deutsch, *Nationalism and Social Communication*, 2d ed. (Cambridge, Mass. and London: M.I.T. Press, 1966); and Leonard Binder, "Nation Building and Political Development," *American Political Science Review* 58 (September 1964): 622–31.

[4] For a cogent presentation of the federalist position, see Carl J. Friedrich, *Trends of Federalism in Theory and Practice* (New York: Praeger, 1968), especially chapters 1 and 2. Also Kenneth C. Wheare, *Federal Government*, 3d ed. (London and New York: Oxford University Press, 1953).

[5] Alternatively, federalism may provide a means of dividing highly centralized authorities in order to provide more decentralization and local autonomy. Donald Rothchild has identified a movement in East Africa from federalism to

that operate successfully at a national level for use on a regional basis. Typically, the successful federation of the original thirteen colonies into the United States of America is depicted as the literal model—albeit a preindustrial one—upon which a United States of Europe can and should be based. But attention is also devoted to other successful federal systems such as Australia, Canada, West Germany, and Switzerland.

Although the federalist notion does have the virtue of heeding political and value orientations, which other theories tend to slight, it leaves something to be desired in its lack of attention to social and economic factors and in its assumption of inherent unities based on historical experience.[6] In terms of practical application, recent experiments in federalism have not been notably successful, as in the case of the abortive federations of Rhodesia and Nyasaland, the British West Indies, Malaysia, Mali, and the United Arab Republic (of Egypt and Syria).[7] And contrary to some basic assumptions of federalism, studies of successful federations reveal that strong centralized institutions of law enforcement and coercion were of only minor importance in their early stages. Thus in the case of Switzerland, the participating cantons retained all military power from the thirteenth to the early nineteenth century. The United States affords another example; it had no War Department until 1798, and even then it possessed a federal army of only 700 men, which was not greatly enlarged for a number of years.[8]

---

neo-federalism as a creative attempt by Kenya, Uganda, and Tanzania to preserve a measure of unity in the face of massive centrifugal pressures. See "From Federalism to Neo-Federalism," in Donald Rothchild, ed., *Politics of Integration: An East African Documentary* (Nairobi, Kenya: East African Publishing House, 1968), p. 10.

[6] On this point see, for example, Ernst B. Haas, "International Integration: The European and the Universal Process," in *International Political Communities: An Anthology* (Garden City, New York: Anchor, 1966), pp. 94–95.

[7] Rothchild has found that political life in the developing areas does not provide the kind of environment conducive to stable federalism. Earlier federal structures in the West were instituted at a time of relative state stability and low citizen demands on government. In addition, constitutionalism and legalism were widely accepted as procedures for the reconciliation of interests. But these conditions are largely absent in the newly independent countries. See "From Federalism to Neo-Federalism," p. 7.

[8] Karl W. Deutsch, Sidney A. Burrell, et al., *Political Community and the North Atlantic Area: International Organization in the Light of Historical Experience* (Princeton, N.J.: Princeton University Press, 1957), pp. 25–26.

Two different theoretical approaches to federalism can be distinguished.[9] One variant, followed by an "activist" group, has aimed at the achievement of regional federations in Western Europe and in Africa. It identifies a popular need that either must necessarily or else ought to lead to a federal outcome. Proponents of this view reject indirect functional means; they prefer the conscious creation of constitutions and formal institutional structures. However, Ernst Haas finds that events in Europe since 1954 and in Africa since 1960 have contradicted and discredited the descriptions, explanations, and predictions of these federalists.[10] An alternative approach to federalism is that of the "theorist" group, which is more concerned with observing patterns of federal integration, although its members have also been active in the writing of constitutions. While they stress the importance of institutional and constitutional questions more than the neo-functionalists do, their characterizations of federalism as a process, or an evolving pattern of relationships, bears resemblance to the ensemble of demands, expectations, bargaining, and growth of institutions on an ad hoc basis with which the neo-functionalists are concerned.[11]

II. Functionalism

As opposed to the federalist conception, it is functional integration that has received the greatest theoretical attention in recent years. The basic statement of functionalism comes from David Mitrany's 1943 work entitled A Working Peace System.[12] Mitrany began by assuming the need for some new kind of international system to replace the one whose breakdown had led to two world wars. He argued that federalism would

---

[9] This distinction is drawn by Ernst Haas in a highly perceptive analysis of the federalist approach. See "The Study of Regional Integration: Reflections on the Joy and Anguish of Pretheorizing," *International Organization* 24 (Autumn 1970): 624–25.

[10] Ibid. Haas identifies Denis de Rougemont, Hans Nord, and Henri Brugmans as partisans of this approach.

[11] Ibid., p. 625. Haas cites in particular the recent work of Carl J. Friedrich.

[12] David Mitrany, *A Working Peace System: An Argument for the Functional Development of International Organization* (London: Oxford University Press, for the Royal Institute of International Affairs, 1943).

not be the best framework for such a new international order because it could not overcome the forces of nationalism and ideology. Even if a number of federal units could be constructed, this would leave the world still divided on a competitive basis. In seeking a pragmatic and global solution, Mitrany put the case for the "Functional Alternative." Peaceful change would come not through a shift of national boundaries but by means of actions taken across them. States would not surrender formal sovereignty—which they certainly remained reluctant to do in any case—but would transfer executive authority for specific ends. World peace could best be promoted if international activities were to be organized around basic functional needs such as transportation, health and welfare necessities, scientific and cultural activities, trade, and even production. There would be as many international organizations as needs, and they would be organized on a universal rather than a regional basis, with countries being under no compulsion to join. Although the immediate outlook was not propitious for political union, functional union would allow all states to work together without such a general political authority. The successful performance of functional activities by bodies that had taken over specific tasks and authorities from governments would bring nations closer together and build a common interest in peace. Instead of engaging in controversies over political schemes, states could easily take part in working arrangements that involved practical "household" tasks. As governments ceded more and more of their tasks to these worldwide organizations, economic unification would not only promote a working peace, but would build the foundations for broader political agreement as well.

During the 1950s Ernst Haas developed a modified version of Mitrany's functionalism in studying the operation of the European Coal and Steel Community.[13] The essence of functionalism, for Haas, was that step-by-step economic decisions were superior to crucial political choices. He held that the operation of ever more controversial policies, starting from a shared interest in economic

[13] Mitrany's thought differs from present functionalist theory in certain respects, especially in his stress upon functional organizations that are universal rather than regional in their membership. For a comparison of Mitrany and Haas, see Andrew W. Green, "Mitrany Reread with the Help of Haas and Sewell," *Journal of Common Market Studies* 8 (September 1969): 50–69. The approach of Haas and his followers is frequently termed "neo-functionalism," but the label of "functionalism" will be retained here.

welfare, would ultimately bring about the establishment of a new supranational authority regardless of the wishes of the individual actors. Haas' functionalism assumed that economic self-interest was more important than political commitment and that unintended consequences and incremental decision making were more effective in bringing about integration than purposive behavior and the construction of elaborate grand designs. In Haas' words, "the determinism implicit in the picture of the European social and economic structures is almost absolute. Given all these conditions, . . . the progression from a politically inspired common market to an economic union, and finally to a political union among states is automatic." [14]

Perhaps the key assumption here was that in modern democratic industrial society, particularly that of Western Europe, there was no longer a distinctly political function, which was separate from economics, welfare, or education, and which existed in the realm of foreign policy, defense and constitution-making. The development of European supranationality was said to symbolize "the victory of economics over politics," thus signaling the demise of the ethnocentric nationalism that preferred guns to butter, passion to reason, and excited demands to statistical bargaining.[15] Common values of productive expansion held sway over those of national interest and ideology. Economic self-interest had become more important than ideological commitment and had brought about economic ties across national boundaries. Decisions arising on an incremental basis produced unintended consequences that furthered the process of integration. Thus a natural economic progression had led the six members of the European Economic Community (EEC) from their initial common community treatment of coal and steel (in the European Coal and Steel Community) to refrigerator tariffs and then to chickens, to monetary policy and ultimately to a mutual interest in the operation of the business cycle.

The notion of functionalism rests on a pluralistic thesis, whereby a larger political community can be developed if crucial expectations, ideologies and behavior patterns of certain key groups can be successfully refocused on a new set of central symbols and institu-

[14] "The 'Uniting of Europe' and the Uniting of Latin America," *Journal of Common Market Studies* 5 (June 1967): 327.
[15] Haas, "Technocracy, Pluralism and the New Europe," in Stephen Graubard, ed., *A New Europe?* (Boston: Houghton Mifflin, 1964), p. 71.

tions.[16] Once crucial tasks are given to a supranational body, the interdependence of economic processes will produce pressure for the granting of further supranational powers involving regulation and adjustment in order to meet successfully the tasks required by the initial shift of powers. Thus within western Europe, agreements involving limited economic sectors produce increased trade flows and common problems. A supranational bureaucracy develops to deal with them, and an increasing number of economic activities are affected by this growing supranational jurisdiction. This leads to what is perhaps Haas' chief finding: as pressure groups begin to organize across national boundaries in order to be able to influence policy decisions that were once the monopoly of national governments, but that now come under the purview of supranational institutions, group pressures "spill over into the federal sphere and thereby add to the integrative impulse." [17] Organized groups, particularly in industry and agriculture, orient themselves toward the community institutions in order to advance their own interests. Over time, the centers of supranational jurisdiction are granted increasing powers, and political loyalties, following the path of economic interest, gradually attach themselves to the new supranational entities.[18] Ultimately, as the result of a shift in economic management and welfare functions, political integration will occur; a supranational body thus supplants the nation-states as the object of secular loyalties.

Although the functionalist theory of integration developed out of the postwar experience of Western Europe, the value of such a theory for broader use in international relations depends in part upon its general applicability. Efforts have been made to apply functionalist theory to such other geographic areas as Latin America (the Latin American Free Trade Area), East Africa (the East

[16] Haas defines integration as "the process whereby political actors in several discrete national settings are persuaded to shift their loyalties and political activities toward a new center whose institutions possess or demand jurisdiction over the pre-existing national states." Ernst B. Haas, *The Uniting of Europe: Political, Social and Economic Forces, 1950–1957* (Stanford: Stanford University Press, 1958), p. 16. Also see Haas, *Beyond the Nation-State: Functionalism and International Organization* (Stanford: Stanford University Press, 1969).
[17] Haas, *The Uniting of Europe* (1968 edition), p. xxxiii.
[18] Roger D. Hansen, "Regional Integration: Reflections on a Decade of Theoretical Efforts," *World Politics* 21 (January 1969): 245.

African Community), and Central America (the Central American Common Market).

Haas himself has cautioned against applying the European model to less developed areas of the world because of substantial differences in key social and economic structures. He does, however, argue that the lessons of the European model remain valid, and that we may be able to utilize these lessons if we can identify functional equivalents for those European features such as national bureaucracies, pragmatic interest groups, parliamentary government and a supranational technocracy.[19]

When functionalist theory of regional integration actually is applied to less developed areas, it produces mostly gloomy conclusions about the likelihood of success in integrative efforts. Integration proceeds fastest when it constitutes a response to socio-economic demands coming from an industrial and urban environment; the factors conducive to regional integration include a pluralist social structure, economic development, and a low level of ideological politics.[20] But these elements are not generally found in underdeveloped regions, where industrialization remains limited and, as a result of the pressures and necessities of nation-building, there is often authoritarian leadership, a one-party political structure, and an emphasis on centralization.

These considerations almost seem to rule out regional integration in a non-European context. And this pessimistic assessment is not limited to any one theoretical approach. Most theories, when applied outside Europe, call attention to such unfavorable factors as national domestic preoccupations, low degrees of administrative skills, lack of sufficient *national* integration, the absence of pluralistic social structures, premature politicization, the highly emotive and symbolic nature of welfare politics, and the excess of domestic loads over "capabilities" for handling them. Indeed, since most theories find that regional integration will not occur in these areas, the more interesting question seems to be why integration has not failed altogether in the underdeveloped world. One suggested answer is that the greater the limits to growth of industrial sectors in smaller

---

[19] " 'The Uniting of Europe' and the Uniting of Latin America," p. 316.
[20] Haas, "International Integration: The European and the Universal Process," pp. 104–105. He also notes that "intensity of integration is positively correlated with industrialization and economic diversification," p. 117.

underdeveloped countries, the more significant is the pressure for progress by means of economic integration.[21] In other words, the necessity for the material benefits of integration may be so compelling as to force nations into integrative efforts regardless of the inappropriateness of certain background conditions. The fact that regional integration somehow occurs, endures, and even advances despite great difficulties provides little comfort for those theories that could not predict or account for such developments. And, if we do heed the cautionary note that we should hesitate to apply the functionalist model to such areas as Latin America, the Middle East and Southeast Asia,[22] this constitutes a definite restriction on the applicability and usefulness of integration theory.

In light of these difficulties of broader application, and particularly with the benefit of the lengthening European experience, functionalist theory has undergone continuous reexamination and modification.[23] To begin with, Haas has acknowledged that the process of economic integration does not lead automatically to political unity. Instead, integration and disintegration exist as two rival social processes simultaneously at work. It was erroneous to assume the permanent superiority of step-by-step economic decisions over crucial political choices and to find an almost absolute determinism in the European social and economic structure.

In 1958, economic advantage proved to be an acceptable shared goal among the six countries of the EEC, and their commitment to supranational integration at first seemed to imply a kind of inevitable movement to de facto political unity. What mattered was not so much fear of the Soviet Union nor envy of the United States, nor slogans of Charlemagne and of Western Civilization; instead it was economic advantage. In Haas' words, "Men thought in terms of realizing the welfare state, of trimming world commitments and an independent foreign policy to the economic and the fiscal demands of domestic welfare. Economics and politics became intermingled, and only a Churchill or a de Gaulle could keep the older vision of high politics alive."[24] Although federalism had been the initial

---

[21] Hansen, "Regional Integration," pp. 262–69. Also see Haas, "International Integration: The European and the Universal Process," p. 126.

[22] Haas, *The Uniting of Europe* (1968 edition), p. xxxvi.

[23] In particular, see Haas, " 'The Uniting of Europe' and the Uniting of Latin America," his preface to the 1968 edition of *The Uniting of Europe*, and his essay, "The Study of Regional Integration."

[24] Haas, " 'The Uniting of Europe' and the Uniting of Latin America," p. 322.

"watchword" in the late 1940s and early 1950s, no effective European federal institutions had been established. The failure of ambitious schemes for the Council of Europe, European Defense Community and European Political Community attested to this fact. Instead, practical functional goals were the means by which European unity was being built. From 1958 onward, the EEC moved toward integration on a functional basis. The Commission of the EEC brought about the elimination of tariffs and quantitative restrictions on trade among the six Common Market countries, established a common external tariff, signed foreign commercial agreements, negotiated for the six in General Agreement on Tariffs and Trade, achieved uniform rules of competition and of industrial concentration, established common agricultural rules and a social fund to finance worker retraining, and initiated regional economic forecasting and efforts at regional monetary policy. Indeed, EEC activities had come close to voiding the powers of national states in all but the areas of defense, education and foreign policy.[25]

Nevertheless, the actions of President de Gaulle taught the functionalists (and the Eurocrats) that nationalism and antifunctional high politics could transcend the measured advances that European integration had made. De Gaulle's veto of Britain's Common Market entry in 1963 and 1967, and his maneuvers to preserve national veto power in order to prevent the initiation of majority voting within the Common Market during 1965 revealed that pragmatic interest politics had built-in limits and that it was vulnerable to political intervention.[26]

Functionalist theory did correctly predict certain kinds of international and interest group behavior. However, that behavior failed to bring about the foreseen integrative political consequences because functionalism, at least for Western Europe, erroneously assumed the end of ideology and overlooked the importance of the external world.[27] Nevertheless, because of its success in describing particular types of European behavior, Haas still asserts the basic soundness of his theory and he maintains that, subject to amendments, the expansive logic of functionalism remains valid. Although he acknowledges that integrative decisions based on high politics

---

[25] Ibid., pp. 323–24.

[26] See, e.g., John Newhouse, *Collision in Brussels: The Common Market Crisis of 30 June 1965* (New York: W. W. Norton, 1967).

[27] Haas, *The Uniting of Europe* (1968 edition), pp. xiii–xv.

are more durable, Haas argues that, in the absence of a statesman (a Bismarck or a Cavour) with the vision to weld disparate publics together, "we have no alternative if we wish to integrate a region, but to resort to gradualism, to indirection, to functionalism." [28]

And yet, even understood in these amended terms, and subject to explicit limitations, functionalist theory faces persistent problems in its application. Although Haas has modified his dismissal of the political function, functionalism does characterize the relation between economic and political union as a continuum. It originally viewed political factors as subordinate to economic ones, so that divergent foreign policy beliefs were regarded as less important than a common commitment to productive expansion. And functionalism continues to imply that a kind of benign invisible hand will operate to bring about supranational integration in a nonideological, depoliticized economic setting. But no more than in the realm of economics can the successful operation of such a laissez-faire process be regarded as inevitable. The point is that a "painless transcendence" of the nation-state is most unlikely without conscious political intervention. [29]

Functionalist theory has viewed depoliticization and a technical treatment of issues as the most promising route to ultimate political integration. Over time, integration was to spill over from the economic to the political sphere as political loyalties followed economic interests and became attached to new supranational institutions. But while "spillover" of integration from one sphere to another does take place in the realm of welfare issues, so that national policies have been modified in industry, trade, agriculture and monetary policy, the operation of politics—"Machiavellian or Bismarckian or Gaullist" [30]—continues to prevail in the arena of high politics. As Stanley Hoffmann incisively observes, this ineradicable political function will persist as long as their exists an international system in which there is competition among states for power and prestige. Indeed, Hoffmann argues that the conditions of the EEC's initiation were virtually unique because of the temporary decline of European nationalism and the European collapse result-

---

[28] " 'The Uniting of Europe' and the Uniting of Latin America," pp. 327–28; also see pp. 321–23.

[29] See, in particular, Stanley Hoffman, *Gulliver's Troubles, or the Setting of American Foreign Policy* (New York: McGraw-Hill, 1968), pp. 404–5.

[30] Stanley Hoffman, "European Process at Atlantic Cross-purposes," *Journal of Common Market Studies* 3 (February 1965): 90.

ing from World War II. This leads us directly to another dimension of the political problem: the requirements for the initiation of integrative efforts.

Several recent studies make it clear that conscious political decisions are required whenever new integrative initiatives are to come about or the scope of an existing arrangement is to be significantly extended. Thus, during the 1958 transformation of the European community, national political leadership proved to be crucial, particularly in the case of Chancellor Adenauer carrying Germany into the new EEC. The neo-functional model, with its stress upon supranational institutions and the process of spillover, failed to provide an adequate description of the actual transformation from the European Coal and Steel Community (ECSC) to the European Economic Community (EEC).[31] Then, in the case of Britain's policy toward the Common Market, political judgments centering around Prime Minister Macmillan proved to be the *sine qua non* for the British decision to seek entry in 1961. (The circumstances were similar to those surrounding Prime Minister Wilson's application in 1966.) In the British case, policy formation was simply not reducible to a mere interplay between organized interests.[32] Finally, in the examples of de Gaulle's veto of British entry in 1963 (and again in 1967), and his successful opposition to EEC majority rule in 1965–66, we are supplied with further evidence of the overall significance of crucial political actions.

Even with such extensive criticism of the functionalist theory of integration, we are still left with what one of its sharpest critics has termed an empirical theory of considerable analytic power and predictive ambition.[33] Functionalism remains valid within limits. That is, although it cannot cope with the more dramatic kinds of integrative advance, nor with integration outside the advanced industrial context, it does offer a useful tool for making sense of group and national behavior within an existing community. It effec-

---

[31] Leon Lindberg and Stuart Scheingold, *Europe's Would-Be Polity: Patterns of Change in the European Community* (Englewood Cliffs, N.J.: Prentice-Hall, 1970), p. 343. The authors provide a useful differentiation between a major type of integrative advance, which they term "systems transformation," and a more incremental change, which they label as "forward linkage growth" (p. 244).

[32] Robert J. Lieber, "Interest Groups and Political Integration: British Entry Into Europe," *American Political Science Review*, 66 (March 1972).

[33] Hoffmann, "European Process at Atlantic Cross-purposes," p. 85.

tively calls our attention to the way in which integration can grow as an unintended product of incremental decisions; it identifies the spillover process that does operate within the realm of welfare politics; it indicates how integration can thrive despite divergent interests and orientations; and it correctly predicts group behavior across national boundaries. Functionalism offers a useful means for making sense of the complex and sprawling integrative enterprise. It provides organizing concepts and helps us to formulate questions, explanations and even predictions. We are thus considerably better off than if we approached this enterprise with only a critical stance and no theory at all. In other words, even a partially successful theory offers concrete advantages.

III. Communications Theory and Integration Theory

While functionalism presently stands as the best known and most widely used theory of integration, there are other complementary or competing theories that can profitably be used to organize our thoughts about integration. In particular, there is the direct application of communications theory (the elements of which will be treated in chapter four). Most commonly associated with the work of Karl Deutsch, this approach defines integration by the concept of the security community. That is, integration requires the attainment of relationships among countries (or within a given country) that no longer anticipate the possibility of warfare against one another, but instead have attained a sense of community strong enough to assure dependable expectations of peaceful change.[34] It is important to note that security communities may be of two different kinds. They can be *amalgamated,* in other words consisting of two or more formerly independent entities merged into one larger unit with a common government whether unitary (e.g., the United Kingdom) or federal (e.g., the United States); or they can be *pluralistic,* in which case each government remains legally separate and independent. For example, the United States and Canada have, since the middle of

---

[34] Deutsch, et al., *Political Community and the North Atlantic Area,* p. 5.

Interaction ——> Integration

the nineteenth century, been "integrated" (in the sense of no longer considering the possibility of warfare against each other), and are therefore categorized as a pluralistic security community. Canada + US

The communications approach applies principles from cybernetics to the relations between nations or population groups. It focuses on the volume of transactions among these entities as the most appropriate indicator, and it operates on the assumption that "cohesiveness among individuals can be measured, and is probably promoted, by the extent of mutual relationship or interaction among them." [35] By focusing on the flow of social transactions among different units, it obtains measurements that are regarded as objective, and that facilitate the making of judgments about the condition of integration.

Several indicators are commonly used; they involve such things as mail flows, telephone traffic, trade figures, and student exchanges. Thus, for example, based on reports of the Universal Postal Union, it is possible to compute for a given country the ratio of domestic to foreign mail (the D/F ratio).[36] This can provide a useful indicator of trends in national versus international preoccupation, and of the ties among two or more countries. Another basic measurement can be constructed from figures for long distance telephone calls. A formula exists for roughly predicting the frequency of calls between two points in a country, say New York and Cleveland, if the figures are known for the number of calls between New York and Chicago.[37] What is interesting here is that the formula will not operate successfully if applied between New York and Montreal. The geo-political fact of the United States–Canadian border is reflected in social transactions as well, so that proportionately fewer phone calls take place between the two countries than within them. By inference, the use of figures such as these, especially if attention were paid to yearly trends, would provide useful data on the extent to which separate countries such as France and Germany were becoming more integrated over time, as well as on how this compared with other groups of integrated countries and with domestic patterns.

---

[35] Philip Jacob and Henry Teune, "The Integrative Process," p. 23.

[36] Karl W. Deutsch, "Transaction Flows as Indicators of Political Cohesion," in Jacob and Toscano, *The Integration of Political Communities,* p. 80.

[37] The formula is "$K = PQ/D^2$, where P and Q are the relevant populations, . . . D is a measurement of distance, and K is a relevant constant." Ibid., p. 82.

Still another indicator exists in the form of a trade matrix. This treats the relative acceptance by countries of each others' exports. Here too, discernible patterns arise that supplement our information and impressions about links between countries and trends over decades or even centuries.

It may seem overly mechanical, or perhaps crude, to focus upon such phenomena as mail flow, telephone calls and trade figures in order to infer conclusions about international politics. However, the approach is justifiable provided certain assumptions are kept in mind. Deutsch takes pains to caution that no one index is adequate by itself. Instead, an ensemble of indices is required, so that if a number of these point in the same direction, for example by signaling an increasing propensity toward mutual attention between France and England, we may then say with some assuredness that underlying social factors are shifting in such a way as to create favorable opportunities for integration. Nor are we concerned exclusively with the raw volume of transactions, since we pay attention to ratios and proportions of total volume. Finally, we are directed to examine the nature of joint rewards and penalties in these transactions. In other words, is a high level of exchange between two peoples accompanied by mutual benefits? If what is good for one side is good for the other—which is often the case in high levels of mutual trade—then we speak of a high covariance of rewards. The existence of this pattern of objective interests, in the presence of a high level of transactions, leads groups to identify with each other; this in turn is expected to bring about greater cohesion between them. On the other hand, if there is a low covariance of rewards, so that what is good for one side is bad for the other, then a high level of contact is not only unlikely to bring about mutual responsiveness, but may even cause conflict.

With these understandings (that several indices must be examined, that trends and ratios rather than the raw volume of transactions are important, and that the mutual covariance of rewards must be scrutinized), we have a highly useful tool at our disposal. The measurement of transaction flows allows us to acquire impersonal evidence in order to test general beliefs, statements, or conclusions about nationalism and political integration. Such a tool surely provides advantages over impressionistic approaches that simply assert: "There is something of interest, I think it means *this*," versus "No, I look at it a different way and I think it means *that*."

Used along with more general understanding, historical information, and personal insights, rather than as a substitute for them, the measurement that the communications approach permits facilitates description, explanation, and even prediction about political integration.

A good example of what applied systematic thinking about integration can achieve is the historical analysis of the integration experience of nearly a dozen countries. Karl Deutsch, Sidney Burrell, et al., in their work, *Political Community and the North Atlantic Area,* drew from several centuries of Western experience in order to abstract those conditions most necessary for the creation and maintenance of political integration. The study examined the experience of English–Scottish Union, the collapse of union between Ireland and the United Kingdom, the growth of German unity from the Middle Ages to 1871, Italian unity in the eighteenth and nineteenth centuries, preservation and dissolution of the Hapsburg Empire, the union and separation of Norway and Sweden, the gradual integration of Switzerland prior to 1848, English–Welsh union after 1485, the formation of England itself, and finally the union of the American Colonies into the United States in 1789 followed by breakup in the Civil War and the subsequent reunion. A total of sixteen shorter-run situations were derived from the above cases.

This study questioned a number of popular beliefs about integration. One such belief was that modern life is somehow more international. Based on figures for trade ratios, immigration patterns and mail flow, the authors found evidence that this was not the case. They also found that no modern industrial state had ever amalgamated with another. A second common belief that the findings contradicted was the idea that there exists a kind of snowball process so that the size of national units is ever increasing. Thus the authors point to such contrary cases as the inability of the United Kingdom to maintain its grip on the American colonies or even on Ireland, the collapse of the Hapsburg Empire, and the dissolution of union between Norway and Sweden. Next, their analysis permits them to challenge the belief that force has operated as an important factor in stimulating integration. Historically, problems of policing and coercion rarely played a large role, and military conquest proved to be one of the least effective methods of integration. Finally, and in contrast to still another widely held notion, they determined that even such a feature as ethnic or linguistic assimilation did not constitute an essential background condition for political integration.

Nine essential conditions for establishment of an amalgamated security community were found to exist. The separate entities had to have mutual compatibility of values, a distinctive way of life, the expectation of stronger economic ties or gains, a marked increase in political and administrative capabilities, superior economic growth, unbroken links of social communication, broadening of political elites, mobility of persons, and a multiplicity of ranges of communication and transaction. Additional conditions were found to be of possible importance; perhaps the most significant one of these was mutual predictability of behavior.[38] Among the more interesting conclusions, the authors found that while both amalgamated and pluralistic security communities constituted practical means to integration, and both exhibited many successful cases, pluralism had particular advantages. Most notably, there was only one case of failure involving a pluralistic security community (that of Austria and Prussia in the German Confederation), whereas there were numerous examples of failure involving amalgamated security communities (e.g., the United States in 1861, Norway-Sweden in 1905, Austria-Hungary in 1917, England-Ireland in 1918, and Metropolitan France with a number of wars and revolutions from 1789 to 1871). Although there are limits to the application of the pluralistic model, its relevance seems to be that in seeking to bring about lasting peaceful relationships among countries, there may be a greater payoff in concentrating efforts upon the less ambitious pluralistic pathway, rather than gambling upon the more elaborate but less probable amalgamated alternative. In other words, pluralistic security communities remain preferable to amalgamated security communities because they are easier to form and less likely to lead to internal conflict.

By dealing with the situations in which political integration actually failed, the study managed to identify a set of background conditions necessary (though perhaps not sufficient in themselves) for disintegration. Examining the failures of England-Ireland, Norway-Sweden, and three separate situations involving Austria, the authors found that these conditions could be divided into two categories: those that increased the burdens on amalgamated gov-

---

[38] Deutsch, et al., *Political Community and the North Atlantic Area*, pp. 57–58.

ernments, and those that reduced the capabilities of governments or political elites for timely response. Under the first category, the authors identified excessive military commitments, a substantial increase in political participation by groups or regions once passive, and an increase in ethnic or linguistic differentiation. Within the second category they placed the conditions of economic decline or stagnation, closure of the political elite (thus promoting the rise of a frustrated counter elite), excessive delay in expected reforms, and major failure of a strong group or region to adjust.

Once again, a systematic effort to deal with the subject matter of international relations suggests a means for improving our grasp of politics. In this case, the indicators of disintegration provide a possible way of organizing our knowledge and even of predicting possible future events of real consequence. For although the authors do not attempt to do so, their criteria can, for example, be employed in examining the contemporary situation of the United States. For nearly a decade, America has lived with a sense of national crisis. Political dialogue, the media, and private conversation have become saturated with statements of the national predicament. But how much does this theme owe to a certain fashionableness of expression, and how are we to judge just how substantial a problem there may be? Will the United States muddle through as in the case of past national difficulties, or is the present situation so different as to be uniquely ominous? Impressionistic statements abound as to problems of race, poverty, violence, drugs, the cities, the universities, and the environment. But can the actual degree of difficulty be analyzed with some precision? Specifically, what possibility is there that America, or at least its political system, might actually disintegrate, i.e., that there might be a breakdown of peaceful political community? There are historical precedents for raising the question and the above criteria provide a method for answering it systematically. By testing the situation of the United States against each of several indicators, it is possible to gauge the nature of the contemporary predicament, compare it with past experience, and make predictions about the future.

In carrying out this analysis, it is clear that all three conditions reflecting burdens or loads upon the government show serious increases throughout the decade of the 1960s. First, military commitments, particularly in the form of the Vietnam War, have been substantial. While the economic costs or (more importantly) the loss of human lives have not been nearly so severe as in World War

II, their duration and political impact do impose an obvious burden.[39] Second, there has been a substantial increase in political participation by formerly passive groups. Most notably by the blacks and other racial minorities, but also on the part of students, anti-war activists, women and Wallace voters. A demonstration, or even a riot, is, after all, a form of political participation, but prior to the 1960s participation by these strata was far less evident. This brings us to the third condition, that of ethnic or linguistic differentiation. Here, the nascent black or Mexican-American movements for increased self-awareness and even separatism are obvious examples. Less obvious, but no less valid in this category, are other groups whose differentiation is such that a sense of community may no longer exist between them and the broader political entity. Here again, portions of the youth, advocates of the counter-culture, and various political extremists of left and right, are clearly differentiated. The extent of these differences is important because Deutsch et al. had identified the ability to communicate, or a sense of "we-feeling," as a definite requirement for successful integration.

If the above conditions reflect sharply increased burdens, what then do the capabilities for meeting these appear to be? Here, the picture is less obvious. To begin with, the economic situation was one of rapid and sustained growth throughout most of the 1960s. For all the inequities, environmental consequences, and later difficulties stemming from budgetary consequences of the Vietnam War, the real standard of living of most Americans rose during this period, and only reached stagnation during the recession of 1970–71 (at a time of slightly reduced political turmoil). Next there is the question of elite closure. Here the picture may be slightly less satisfactory, as the various political, administrative, and business elites perhaps have offered only a limited accessibility to newly mobilized strata. Related to this, there does appear to be excess delay in expected reforms. To a certain extent, the problem may be

---

[39] Defense spending as a percentage of Gross National Product was 8.1 percent in 1965, 9.1 percent in 1966, 10.2 percent in 1967, and approximately 10.2 percent in 1968. Yet at the height of the Vietnam War, the *relative* defense spending was within the range of the peacetime years of 1954–64, in which costs ranged from a high of 12.9 percent (1954) to a low of 8.7 percent (1964). The range for the Korean War years of 1951–53 was 10.9 percent to 14.9 percent. The peak in World War II was over 40 percent. *Source:* Bruce M. Russett, *What Price Vigilance?* (New Haven, Conn. and London: Yale University Press, 1970), pp. 104 and 132.

one of a revolution of rising expectations, but the fact is that the response of the political system has not been perceived as effective when contrasted with the magnitude of the problems facing it. (Here, the burden of military commitments may have had its most serious effect.) Finally, has there been a major failure of a strong group to adjust? In this case, we must include those groups whose political mobilization and differentiation made up the burdens upon the political system. In addition, there may be further difficulties of adjustment as a consequence of both technological innovation and the changes wrought by those efforts that are made to deal with the above problems. Thus elements of the celebrated "silent majority," white ethnic groups, blue collar workers, businessmen, teachers, and military leaders, as well as some students, blacks, and the poor may resist adjustment to either the status quo or to innovations in it.

From this overview, one conclusion may be that the strongest element in favor of persistent national integration is the economy; indeed, prosperity may operate as a kind of social cement. The prediction could follow that the overall situation will remain manageable so long as the economy stays healthy. The United States would thereby be able to maintain a balance of capabilities over burdens. However, were the United States to falter into an economic predicament as serious as the depression of the 1930s, on top of the present social problems, burdens might then outdistance capabilities and the picture would become truly ominous. The use of the disintegration indicators has thus permitted us to gain a measure of perspective on a complex and sprawling situation; it also suggests the importance of economic prosperity, which might not otherwise have been so obvious. Indeed, not only has this exercise enabled us to analyze and make tentative predictions, but it also produces criteria for significant policy recommendations. In this case, the importance placed on sustaining the health of the economy could be translated into recommendations that such needs take precedence over military or space commitments, and perhaps that the government ought to pay careful attention to maintaining employment at a level as high as possible, even at a cost of some inflation, budget deficit, or international financial difficulty.

There is of course room for criticism here, both of the North Atlantic study and of the above application of the disintegration criteria. For one thing, the North Atlantic study treated societies that were mostly preindustrial, for another, the United States would hardly be likely to fragment along state or geographic lines as it did in the Civil War. Of course, one answer to these criticisms is that while we cannot be sure whether the present highly industrial circumstances might indeed limit the applicability of the study, some of the historical examples involved at least an early industrial period. More directly, the disintegration need not be regarded in geographic terms; the communications method seems to suggest that the existence of separate and possibly antagonistic groups unable or unwilling to communicate with one another could indeed produce lines of civil fragmentation.

Just as there are basic criticisms of functionalism, so the communications approach has received its share of challenges. The most common argument is that because the content of messages is not specified, the attention to transactions is far too crude and nonpolitical. In fact, as ought to have been clear from the above discussion, this misses the point. Transaction indicators such as mail flow, tourist exchanges, and the rate of supranational group formation are not treated as individual answers in themselves. Instead, they are examined as an ensemble, and in combination with other information about the relationship in question. One analogy, aptly employed by Deutsch, is of the use by a doctor of a patient's bloodcount in making a diagnosis. A bloodcount by itself would be of little value, since a given result could signify radically different states of health or illness. Instead, the doctor analyzes the bloodcount in conjunction with his knowledge of the patient's past medical history and present symptoms, and in addition incorporates his own medical knowledge. The indicator involved is thus a highly useful tool when combined with these other factors. So too, the figures for transaction ratios can be a useful element in a broader analytic enterprise.

There are, however, two other criticisms of the communications approach that are more valid. The first of these asks what precisely the communications approach seeks to explain. In other words, what is the dependent variable? If the focus of attention is merely upon the pluralistic security community, this approach may be of limited use, for Western Europe has constituted such an arrangement since soon after the Second World War, and concentration upon this relationship may not tell us very much. If instead there is a basic concern with political unity (and the Deutsch approach has dealt at length with the contemporary nature and prospects of European unity), then this concern could be made more explicit. There is a second criticism. It asks whether an intensive pattern

It a came?

of transactions must actually bring about closer integration, or whether the communications pattern is more loosely correlated with the establishment of political community so that the two phenomena do not necessarily increase or decline together (i.e., that they do not necessarily *covary*). This question is perhaps not yet answerable, but it is raised because the main prediction of the communications approach has been that the future integration of Europe is likely to stagnate for at least a generation as a result of the leveling off of transaction rates after 1957.

IV. Measuring Integration

Several recent efforts have been made to obtain specific measurements of integration in the European context. While each of these remains somewhat qualified and tentative, they represent stimulating enterprises in their attempt to join quantitative precision to more grand theoretical underpinnings. In the case of the communications approach, Deutsch and Edinger have judged that intraEuropean transactions, after dramatically increasing for over a decade, have slowed since the mid 1950s and have come to rest on a kind of plateau since 1957–58.[40] This conclusion is based on the evidence of several indicators. First, an examination of mutual preferences of the six Common Market countries for dealing with one another rather than with other countries (as measured by trade, mail flow, travel, and student exchanges) shows that while Europe is much more integrated than at any time between the world wars or even prior to 1914, there has been no increase in most of these indicators of integration since the early 1950s. Thus for example, the relative acceptance of each other's exports among the six actually peaked in 1948–51. Indeed, when compared with the postwar pattern for Scandinavia and for the United States and Canada, where the relative acceptances are from two to four times greater, the trade figures indicate how relatively limited the actual integration of European trade has been. (See Figure 3-1). Next, a content analysis of news-

---

[40] Karl W. Deutsch, Lewis J. Edinger, Roy C. Macridis, and Richard L. Merritt, *France, Germany and the Western Alliance: A Study of Elite Attitudes on European Integration and World Politics* (New York: Scribners, 1967), see especially chapter 13.

FIGURE 3-1

Regional Relative Acceptance Scores
For International Trade, 1890–1963

Year	The Six	Anglo-America *	Scandinavia	Canada-United States	United States-Canada
1890	.40	.63	11.89	3.73	3.25
1913	.30	.63	6.26	3.59	4.39
1928	.57	.36	5.30	1.81	3.13
1938	.62	.40	2.69	2.15	3.46
1948	1.07	.10	3.06	2.1	1.9
1954	.79	.45	2.73	2.85	2.93
1957	.82	.48	2.28	3.2	2.2
1959	.83	.49	2.99	2.7	2.3
1963	.77	.53	3.89	2.6	2.5

* The "Anglo-American region" includes Britain, Canada, Ireland and the United States, that is, all English-speaking counties in the North Atlantic area.

Source: Karl Deutsch, Lewis J. Edinger, Roy C. Macridis, and Richard L. Merritt, France, Germany and the Western Alliance (New York: Scribners, 1967), p. 222.

paper editorials, for example, in *Le Monde* and the *Frankfurter Allgemeine Zeitung*, reveals no significant growth in the frequency of references to Europeanism during the years from 1953 to 1963. Finally, studies of elite and mass public opinion indicate that national issues remain more important than European ones. A case in point is West Germany, where 51 percent of the West Germans felt, in 1965, that the most important task facing their country was "national reunification," whereas only 3 percent named European union.[41] Indeed, Deutsch and Edinger found specific European nationality anywhere from two to ten times more powerful as a determinant of attitudes toward European questions than cross-national factors such as social class, age, religion, party or ideology.[42] Taken together, these various streams of data indicate that rates of

[41] Karl W. Deutsch, "Integration and Arms Control in the European Environment: A Summary Report," *American Political Science Review* 60 (June 1966): 357.

[42] Ibid., p. 364. This means that, for example, French Socialists are still Frenchmen first and Socialists second.

European social assimilation have stagnated or even declined slightly. From this fact, Deutsch concludes that there is a low probability of political integration in Western Europe during the next couple of decades.

These conclusions are, however, directly challenged by the functionalists, particularly Leon Lindberg and Ernst Haas, who argue that it is since 1957 that European integration has made its "greatest strides." [43] Lindberg constructs a numerical measurement for the extent of political community. Employing an idea of William Riker's, he establishes point scores on the basis of where decisions are made. On one end of the scale, a point value of "1" applies to decisions that would be entirely centralized (i.e., made wholly within the European Community system); point values rise with increasing decentralization until the other end of the scale is reached where there is a value of "7" for those decisions made entirely by individual states. [44] Lindberg then applies this scale to seventeen different functions, including areas such as external affairs, patriotism, education, health, money, and resources. The result (Figure 3-2), which is meant to be illustrative rather than conclusive, shows an average of 6 for the year 1966. For 1970, Lindberg calculated an increase in

---

[43] Leon N. Lindberg, "The European Community as a Political System: Notes Toward the Construction of a Model," *Journal of Common Market Studies* 5 (June 1967): 344. Also see Lindberg, *The Political Dynamics of European Economic Integration* (Stanford: Stanford University Press, 1963), and Ernst B. Haas, "Technocracy, Pluralism and the New Europe," in Stephen A. Graubard, ed., *A New Europe?*

[44] His full scale of decision locus reads as follows:

1. Decisions are taken entirely in the European Community system.
2. Decisions are taken almost entirely in the European Community system.
3. Decisions are taken predominantly in the European Community system, but the nation-states play a significant role in decision making.
4. Decisions are taken about equally in the European Community system and the nation-states.
5. Decisions are taken predominantly by the nation-states, but the European Community system plays a significant role in decision-making.
6. Decisions are taken almost entirely by the nation-states.
7. Decisions are taken entirely by the nation-states individually.

Lindberg, "The European Community as a Political System," pp. 356–57. More elaborate calculations of the scope of the European Community can be found in Lindberg and Scheingold, *Europe's Would-Be Polity*, chapter 3; and in Lindberg's "Political Integration as a Multidimensional Phenomenon Requiring Multivariate Measurement," *International Organization* 24 (Autumn 1970): 649–731.

FIGURE 3-2

Index of Extent of the Political Community: The EEC in 1966 and 1970

	1966	1970
1. External affairs	7	6
2. Public safety	7	7
3. Property rights	6	6
4. Civic rights	7	7
5. Morality	7	7
6. Patriotism	7	6
7. Education	7	6
8. Recreation	7	7
9. Knowledge	7	6
10. Health	6	6
11. Indigency	6	5
12. Utilities		
a. energy	5	3
b. water supply, sewerage, etc.	7	7
13. Money and credit		
a. currency	7	6
b. domestic credit	7	5
c. balance of payments	5	4
d. current financing	6	6
14. Production and distribution		
a. agriculture	3	3
b. labor-management relations	6	6
c. industrial competition	5	4
d. tariffs and quotas	2	1
15. Economic development	6	5
16. Transport and communication	6	4
17. Resources	6	6
Average	6	5.37

Source: Leon N. Lindberg, "The European Community as a Political System: Notes Toward the Construction of a Model," Journal of Common Market Studies 5 *(June 1967): 359.*

integration, with an estimated figure of 5.37; in other words, slow but measurable progress toward integration.

The scale also permits a comparison with the extent of political community in Central America and East Africa (Figure 3-3). It

FIGURE 3-3

Index of Extent of the Political Community: A Comparison of Western Europe, Central America and East Africa [a]

	EEC 1966	Central America 1966	East Africa 1960	East Africa 1963	East Africa 1966
1. External affairs	7	5	1	6	6
2. Public safety	7	7	4	7	7
3. Property rights	6	7	5	7	7
4. Civic rights	7	7	5	7	7
5. Morality	7	7	7	7	7
6. Patriotism	7	7	5	7	7
7. Education	7	6	4	4	5
8. Recreation	7	7	7	7	7
9. Knowledge	7	6	5	6	6
10. Health	6	6	6	6	6
11. Indigency	6	7	7	7	7
12. Utilities					
a. energy	5	7	6	6	6
b. water supply, sewerage, etc.	7	7	7	7	7
13. Money and credit					
a. currency	7	6	1	2	6
b. domestic credit	7	7	3	3	6
c. balance of payments	5	5	2	4	6
d. current financing	6	7	4	5	6
14. Production and distribution					
a. agriculture	3	6	6	6	6
b. labor management	6	6	6	6	6
c. industrial competition	5	6	6	6	6
d. tariffs and quotas	2	3	1	1	3
15. Economic development	6	6	5	5	6
16. Transport and communication	6	6	3	3	4
17. Resources	6	7	7	7	7
Average	6.0	6.3	4.7	5.5	6.0

[a] A low score indicates that nearly all decisions in a field are taken by the group as a whole, while a high score of seven indicates that decisions are taken entirely by the nation-states individually.

Source: Joseph S. Nye, "Comparative Regional Integration: Concept and Measurement," International Organization, 21 (1968): 870.

allows us to observe that in the early 1960s East Africa was initially more integrated than the EEC, but that by 1966 the extent of integration in the two areas had become similar. And use of the scale provides a means for projecting that European integration will increase further, while African integration declines.

At this point, if we put aside the comparative dimension and concentrate on the various assessments of the EEC, we seem to be faced with two contradictory conclusions based on different kinds of measurement of European integration. The instinctive reaction may therefore be to question the possibility of coming to reliable conclusions about integration itself, let alone any sort of valid measurement. Yet it remains possible to make sense of this by realizing that entirely different dimensions of integration are being assessed by Deutsch and Lindberg. Deutsch is measuring the linking of *peoples,* or international community formation, whereas Lindberg treats the linking of *governments* in supranational institutions and policymaking processes, or international political amalgamation.[45] The former dimension includes such features as the development of mutual trust and predictability, economic integration, and the lowering of communications barriers. It predicts that political amalgamation (the linking of governments) will follow from community formation (the linking of peoples). The latter approach deals with formal institutions, both governmental and nongovernmental, and it holds the reverse, that community formation will come as a result of political amalgamation. What Donald Puchala finds in his comparison of these approaches and measurements, as well as from his own scrutiny of the relationship between France and Germany, is that neither theory of integration is wholly correct. Instead, Puchala claims that international community formation and international political amalgamation are not directly related, and they may even move in different directions. Therefore it was as inappropriate for one group of theorists to conclude that the leveling off of indicators in the linking of peoples would necessarily signal a halt in the integration of institutions as it was for the other group to conclude that progress in the linking of institutions would cause a definite advance in the

---

[45] Donald J. Puchala, "Integration and Disintegration in Franco-German Relations, 1954–1965," in *International Organization* 34 (Spring 1970): 184–85. For another thoughtful classification of the various notions and types of integration into economic, social and political, see Joseph S. Nye, "Comparative Regional Integration," pp. 856–74.

integration of peoples. At the same time, however, community formation was found to provide a significant "endurance" factor to political relations between governments, so that existing supranational arrangements might better be able to withstand occasional crises. In addition, the course of relations between the two key countries in the European enterprise, France and Germany, was predictable from cybernetic postulates: the fragile system of Franco-German intergovernmental coordination became overburdened in the early 1960s and broke down when (due to a series of difficulties over important issues) loads outdistanced capabilities. Presumably, the later decrease in loads would allow us to predict at least the possibility of renewed progress toward integration and political amalgamation.[46]

V. Conclusion: Integration Theory and International Relations

Integration theory has its limitations. Indeed, integration theory itself is not wholly "integrated." It consists of various tentative hypotheses operating at different levels of analysis. On the one hand there are the highly systemic abstractions of the communications approach, on the other hand there are the involved treatments of behavior by the functionalists. There have been only a few tentative efforts to join these separate levels of analysis more directly. In addition, much of the work on integration has dealt with Western Europe, and those studies that have centered on underdeveloped areas have frequently found the existing theoretical notions of limited use outside the European context. Finally, even in the European context, integration theories have been unable to include the impact of external factors upon the integrative process.

Valid criticisms of integration theory should not cause us to lose sight of its very real accomplishments and possibilities. It is a fact

---

[46] Puchala, "Integration and Disintegration," pp. 199–201. Between 1962 and 1965, France and Germany were forced to deal with NATO reform, the proposed multilateral nuclear force (MLF), agricultural problems within the EEC, negotiations over Britain's Common Market entry, and disputes over the powers of the EEC Commission.

that most of the research on political integration has been guided in some way by these theories. This has been so whether the collection of data was undertaken within a larger theoretical framework, or whether it was governed by the wish to test hypotheses in order to support, reject, or criticize a given theoretical position. As a result, a body of evidence and theorizing is emerging that displays an increasing coherence. The integration theories have been of substantial heuristic value. They have permitted an economy of effort, so that studies have dealt with related questions and have built upon one another. They have also stimulated thought and the organization of knowledge.

With its possibilities and limitations, integration theory is in some ways a microcosm of the developing status of international relations theory itself. There is a growing theoretical structure accompanied by an elaborate and sometimes opaque vocabulary, and research and theorizing have become more related and more cumulative. There have been solid accomplishments as well as efforts, errors, and costs, and out of this work a theoretical tool offering considerable analytic power has unmistakably begun to take shape.

BIBLIOGRAPHY

COBB, ROGER W., and CHARLES ELDER. *International Community: A Regional and Global Study.* New York: Holt, 1970. An ambitious effort to consider integration theory systematically. Combines theoretical material with comparative quantitative data.

DEUTSCH, KARL W., SIDNEY BURRELL, et al. *Political Community and the North Atlantic Area.* Princeton, N.J.: Princeton University Press, 1957. An impressive historical study of the conditions involved in the early integration or disintegration of political communities in Western Europe and North America. Utilizes the communications approach to integration theory.

FRIEDRICH, CARL J. *Trends of Federalism in Theory and Practice.* New York: Praeger, 1968. A cogent introduction to the federalist approach, by one of its leading proponents.

HAAS, ERNST. *Beyond the Nation-State: Functionalism and International Organization.* Stanford: Stanford University Press, 1964. A study of the International Labor Organization in light of functionalist theory.

————. *The Uniting of Europe: Political, Social and Economic Forces,*

1950–1957. Stanford: Stanford University Press, 1958. The basic revision and application of functionalist theory to Europe. Deals with the experience of the European Coal and Steel Community. (Preface to the 1968 edition contains an excellent restatement and modification of the author's position.)

International Political Communities: An Anthology. Garden City, New York: Anchor, 1966. A useful collection, containing selections from the major authors and approaches to integration theory.

JACOB, PHILIP, and JAMES TOSCANO, eds. *The Integration of Political Communities*. Philadelphia: Lippincott, 1964. An attempt to apply the communications approach, particularly at the metropolitan level.

KITZINGER, UWE. *The Politics and Economics of European Integration*. New York: Praeger, 1963. An excellent introduction to the origins and development of the movement for European unity.

LIEBER, ROBERT J. *British Politics and European Unity: Parties, Elites, and Pressure Groups*. Berkeley: University of California Press, 1970. Deals with the formulation of British policy toward Europe. Finds distinctly political choices to have been crucial in moving Britain to seek Common Market entry.

LINDBERG, LEON. *The Political Dynamics of European Economic Integration*. Stanford: Stanford University Press, 1963. A functionalist treatment of the operation of the European Economic Community.

LINDBERG, LEON, and STUART SCHEINGOLD. *Europe's Would-Be Polity: Patterns of Change in the European Community*. Englewood Cliffs, N.J.: Prentice-Hall, 1970. An effort to synthesize theories of European integration and of the integration process more generally.

LINDBERG, LEON, and STUART SCHEINGOLD, eds. *Regional Intergration: Theory and Research*. Cambridge, Mass., 1971. A group of significant and original essays appraising achievements and prospects of recent work in this field. (Originally published as a special issue of *International Organization*, Autumn, 1970.)

MITRANY, DAVID. *A Working Peace System*. Chicago: Quadrangle Books, 1966. Contains the succinct and eloquent original statement of functionalism, as well as a number of Mitrany's later writings on international order.

4

Cybernetics

and

Communications

Theory

I. Introduction: Engineering Systems and Human Systems

The application of communications theory to international relations has developed rapidly over the past decade. A number of orientations and bodies of theory exist within the communications field, but the most promising work stems from the ideas of cybernetics and it is upon cybernetics that this chapter will focus.[1]

Although it possesses a compelling utility in the study of politics, cybernetics, like game theory, originated in the work of mathematicians. And like game theory it is also a partial theory that applies to the political behavior of decision-makers and nation-states. Cybernetics itself may be defined as "the systematic study of communication and control in organizations of all kinds. . . . Essentially it represents a shift in the center of interest from drives to steering, and from instincts to systems of decisions, regulation and con-

---

[1] In addition to cybernetics, somewhat less prominent orientations involving mediated stimulus response and cognitive balance also occupy a place in the field of international political communication. For a discussion of these efforts, see Davis Bobrow, "The Transition from International Communication to International Relations as Communication." Paper delivered at the Sixty-Sixth Annual Meeting of the American Political Science Association, Los Angeles, California, September 8–12, 1970.

trol. . . ." [2] The first major formulation of its ideas was put forward by Norbert Wiener in the late 1940s.[3] Wiener had noted major wartime advances in electronic processes such as sonar, radar, radar directed anti-aircraft fire, and transfer of coded messages through advanced communication networks. All of these developments involved some measure of information transfer and self-correction through a feeding back into the decision system of the results of actual system performance. Wiener contended that these communication processes in machines bore a fundamental similarity to individual human, social, and institutional processes. In other words, a basic identity existed in the technical nature of communication, whether the system involved was one employing electronic signals, human nerve cells, or governmental bureaucracy. In the steps by which they operated these entities had a great deal in common: they could receive and send messages, store and reproduce various kinds of data, and draw upon a memory of facts and formulae. Basically, they were goal-oriented systems that shared the ability to select certain kinds of information, combine old and new information, and monitor their own performance. Lest this be regarded as a crude, mechanistic or dehumanizing identification of men with machines, it is well to draw upon Wiener's own carefully stated position:

While human and social communication are extremely complicated in comparison to the existing patterns of machine communication, they are subject to the same grammar; and this grammar has received its highest technical development when applied to the simpler content of the machine.[4]

As Wiener noted, social science is based on the ability to treat a social group as an organization, and "communication is the cement

---

[2] Karl W. Deutsch, *The Nerves of Government: Models of Political Communication and Control* (New York: The Free Press, 1966), p. 76. For Deutsch's important formulation of the cybernetic approach, see especially pp. 75–109 and 182–99.

[3] See his *Cybernetics: Control and Communication in the Animal and the Machine* (Cambridge, Mass.: M.I.T. Press, 1948). Wiener's later work, *The Human Use of Human Beings: Cybernetics and Society* (Boston: Houghton Mifflin, 1950), introduces cybernetics to a wider audience. For an excellent introduction to this work, see the "Afterword" by Walter A. Rosenblith in the 1968 edition of *The Human Use of Human Beings* (London: Sphere Books), pp. 168–77.

[4] Quoted in Deutsch, *The Nerves of Government*, p. 77.

that makes organizations." Therefore, by concentrating upon the communications process itself we will greatly increase our comprehension of how all kinds of organizations actually operate.[5] Indeed, since organizations operate within limits set by their communication, a means of understanding a previously intractable subject may suggest itself. For if something we wish to comprehend is closed to us—perhaps the inner workings of the Soviet Politburo or the mind of a United States president—there may nonetheless be opportunities for gaining greater knowledge of it by regarding the object as a "black box," that is, something for the moment sealed off from direct scrutiny but the inputs and outputs of which are visible.[6] The indirect procedure of focusing on communications and transactions that go into and come out of the black box may ultimately reveal significant information about the contents of the box, for example, the attitudes or procedures of otherwise inaccessible decision-makers, and may even provide insights about decision-making processes themselves. The value of the cybernetic approach is that it opens the possibility of applying techniques borrowed from engineering and electronics to biological and social processes; these human phenomena may then be made more susceptible to quantitative treatment and ultimately to improved understanding.

Karl Deutsch is responsible for the chief development and application of cybernetic theory to international politics. In his view, cybernetics, understood in terms of communication and control, offers a general perspective on *all* politics. Communications are literally the "nerves of government." By directing our attention to such matters as how decisions are made, message flow between decision-makers, message storage and retrieval, and the response of decision-makers, cybernetics may provide significant insights about how and why political systems survive and change.

The cybernetic model also displaced earlier and inadequate classical theoretical conceptions that had persisted for over a cen-

---

[5] Ibid.

[6] The "Problem of the Black Box" is treated in W. Ross Ashby, *An Introduction to Cybernetics* (New York: John Wiley, 1956), pp. 86 ff. It originally arose in electrical engineering, involving a sealed box with terminals for input and output from which an engineer sought to deduce information about its contents. An analogous problem may apply when a clinician seeks to deal with a brain-damaged patient.

tury. Among the most prevalent of these were organic models, based on analogies between the human body and the state. These models left no room for the learning process, did not provide the opportunity for internal rearrangement or accurate analysis, and regarded natural law as providing sufficient explanation for political phenomena. There were also historical models, which did devote a certain amount of attention to growth and innovation but provided no improved understanding of the operation of these processes themselves, nor any possibility of quantitative predictability. Finally, mechanical and equilibrium models tended to present entities whose whole constituted no more than the sum of their parts and whose parts did not modify one another. They gave no opportunity for insights into processes of growth or change, and their application favored a static social theory.[7] Thus in contrast to such earlier models, Deutsch has argued that even as a mere analogy cybernetics would be superior to previous analogies that shaped our theoretical conceptions of politics. Because cybernetics indicates that it is *steering* that stands as the most fundamental process, the study of it in institutions, societies, and individuals ought to increase our grasp of problems in all these fields.

Of equal importance is the possibility that the communications model may provide marked advantages in policy making. John Burton, the leading theorist in this field in Britain, argues that communications models that focus upon decision-making processes are strongly preferable to static concepts of balances and to the traditional power politics point of view that they foster. For Burton, the use of force is a measure of the ability not to have to learn or to adjust or to accept peaceful change, and power is a concept that is used by those with superior might to maintain the status quo. The use of the communications model by policy-makers would increase the possibility of nations being able to understand each other's decision processes and thereby anticipate mutual responses so that the development of certain intolerable options could be prevented. Decision-making models are appropriate to international politics in a nuclear age that demands considerable ability to change goals—especially in the shift from the short-run aim of exclusive

---

[7] John Burton, *International Relations: A General Theory* (New York and London: Cambridge University Press, 1965), p. 147; and Deutsch, *The Nerves of Government,* p. 48.

national security to a longer term preservation of civilization itself—
something not easily managed in power politics terms.[8]

From Burton's viewpoint, power models ignore decision processes
that stem from influences other than power, whereas the communications model concentrates upon national decision processes
so as to determine what influences shape relations between states:

The power-model provides no alternatives to conflict or power politics
in one form or another; a communications model at least points to the
possibilities within decision-making processes of weighing both the
international bargaining options and the internal adjustments.[9]

International political communication analysis thus diverts attention from such phenomena as the history of power balances, the
policies of powerful states, collective security, and the record of
international attempts at achieving world government, to the interplay of national with international politics. Attention is redirected
from power and drives to steering and control. The concern is with
forms of economics, education, ideology and social and political
structures. In Burton's terms the options for nations are to pursue
their national interest on the one hand by action to prevent or
promote change by force, or on the other hand to work toward
adjustment and negotiation.

With some of these initial considerations in mind, let us now
examine the central ideas of cybernetics in more detail, then analyze
the possibilities of their application to international politics.

II. The Central Ideas of
Cybernetics

Cybernetics begins with the very
general concept of a self-controlling system. That is, its attention is
directed to any system that possesses sufficient organization, communication, and control. This applies whether message transmission
is by electronic signals in a computer, human speech or writing in a
society, or nerve impulses within a human body. The basic features

[8] Burton, *International Relations*, pp. 148–49.
[9] Ibid., p. 272.

that these systems share include their nature as networks of information flow; their capacity to receive and recombine new with stored information; their operation as decision-making entities, and their ability to change their performance by taking into account the results of their previous goal-seeking actions.

The key idea in cybernetics is that of *information,* for this is the element that circulates in any communication network. Indeed, cybernetic theorists claim for this commodity a status with other major scientific concepts such as matter, energy and the electric charge.[10] Information can be reproduced, stored, or quantified—hence its accessibility to measurement and its use in international political analysis—but unlike matter or energy it can be both created and destroyed. By measuring the amount of information that is transmitted, lost, or received, we can obtain an index of the efficiency of a communications channel. The importance of information to self-controlling systems is that it enables them to adjust to their environment; its presence is thus the *sine qua non* of system autonomy.

Information is also the negative of *entropy,* another critical concept of cybernetics. Entropy, as a concept, comes from thermodynamics, but the process itself is readily understandable. Basically, entropy is the tendency of a closed system to deteriorate. In thermodynamics this applies particularly to loss of heat, but the broader systemic process involves decay from a more highly organized, differentiated, and less probable state to a less organized, undifferentiated, and more probable or chaotic state. According to Norbert Wiener, both living things and machines, since they represent greater orderliness, are instances of decreasing entropy. In a slightly theological vein, Wiener once observed that science's attempt to discover order in the universe was continually undertaken against a "devil" interpreted as the absence of order.[11] As a more mundane example of entropy, anyone who has ever rented a furnished residence will appreciate the tendency of things to break down, however diligent the attentions of the occupant. Thus the irate landlord, obsessed with a broken chair or suddenly defective plumbing, might be consoled by having his attention called to the theoretical insight that these are instances

---

[10] Wiener, *Human Use of Human Beings,* pp. 175–76.
[11] Cited by Walter A. Rosenblith, "Afterword" to Wiener, *Human Use of Human Beings* (1968 edition), p. 174.

not of tenant negligence but of an ineluctable and universal entropy.[12] Any owner of an automobile will also have experienced at first hand the operation of entropy.

The advantage that human and other information systems possess is their ability to adapt to changes in their surroundings, to continue to learn, and thus to work against the current of entropy. This learning process is contingent upon *feedback*, another fundamental cybernetic concept and certainly the central mechanism in its operation. Feedback itself involves modifying system behavior on the basis of incorporating, or "feeding back" information on the nature of that system's actual, rather than anticipated, performance. The quality of feedback decisively shapes the effectiveness of the system in pursuing its goals. Feedback, which is common to all self-controlling systems, can be based on quantitative indices, the success or failure of some action, or the outcome of an entire behavior syndrome. Thus the information contained therein might deal with the distance by which anti-aircraft fire has missed its target, the relative success of a certain kind of technique in selling used cars (or used tanks), or perhaps the efficacy of a national policy in promoting a country's security. The inputs that these results provide are then the basis—together with stored data or memory—for the system to modify its future actions in order to have a better chance of attaining its goal (whether downed aircraft, sold cars, or national survival). Yet another example of the operation of a feedback mechanism is provided by the management of modern economies, where data on employment, inflation, and industrial production are continually assessed and are the basis for decisions about adjustments in national monetary and fiscal policies.

Feedback may also be of two very different types. On the one hand there is *negative* feedback, in which system behavior is controlled by the margin of error in reference to a specific goal and signals from the goal are used to restrict output. Negative feedback, by reducing a previous action, is thus the essence of goal attainment.[13] On the other hand, *positive* feedback is a very different sort of phenomenon. It involves amplification or reinforcement of exist-

---

12 Unfortunately, in the author's own case these observations produced not philosophical reflection in the presence of a universal phenomenon, but marked acrimony.
13 Deutsch, *The Nerves of Government*, pp. 88–89.

ing behavior; learning to read and escalation of an arms race are two markedly different examples of positive feedback.[14]

The efficiency of the feedback process can be measured by examining four factors.[15] The first of these is called *load*, and has to do with the amount of information a system must process. Typically the concern here is with pressures upon a state's machinery for political decision making. Second, there is *lag*, or the delay between the time information about the location of the "target" is received and the point at which corrective action is carried out. Obviously the more sizeable the system's lag, the less likely it is to attain any changing goal. In political terms, lag measures the delay in response of decision-makers to a new situation of any kind. The third factor is *gain*, or the extent of corrective action actually taken. Too great a corrective action can cause a system to overshoot its goal, just as too limited a gain can allow it to fall short. This index measures the speed and extent of political and governmental reaction time, for example, in terms of political or military mobilization in response to a sudden external challenge. Finally there is *lead*, or the distance of the predicted location of a moving target or goal from its previous position. Just as deer-hunters or anti-ballistic missiles may "lead" their targets, so political systems require the ability to anticipate new problems. Since all governments and communications systems depend on information processing and hence upon feedback, their efficiency can be measured in terms of these four factors. If persistent imbalances develop between the communications loads placed upon political institutions and the capabilities that they possess for coping with these loads, then systems may fail to attain their goals or else suffer serious breakdown.[16] For example, analyzed from the perspective of cybernetics, United States decision making during the Vietnam war was characterized by very poor feedback with regard to such important matters as the impact of bombing

---

[14] In fact, feedback equations have been used very successfully in constructing theoretical models of arms races. Bobrow, "Transition from International Communication," p. 26.

[15] The terms and their application are those of Deutsch, *The Nerves of Government*, pp. 90, 187–91.

[16] Those things that facilitate communication represent capabilities. Such factors as a high degree of mutual attention, a high and wide-ranging array of transactions, and patterns of mutual identification are important in maintaining significant capabilities.

upon the will of North Vietnamese decision-makers and the success of the pacification program. In terms of load, the decision system was inundated with information, some of which was faulty (e.g., reported number of enemy casualties, proportion of "safe" hamlets), information stored in memory was sometimes not drawn upon (e.g., the strategic bombing survey dealing with American air attacks on Germany during World War II), and more cautious assessments (e.g., by the CIA) were disregarded in favor of sanguine judgments.[17] Furthermore, the amplification of ongoing efforts (a form of positive feedback) brought more bombing, more casualties, more refugees, widespread misery, and no real success in the attainment of original goals. Finally, the lag, or delay, of United States decision-makers in responding to the developing Vietnamese situation was also acute, so that it took a long time for the United States to respond to the fact that bombing was having little effect on the fighting abilities of the Viet Cong and North Vietnamese.

III. Communication and Control

The balance between capabilities and loads assumes considerable importance in the analysis of international politics from the cybernetic viewpoint. This measurement itself is dependent upon the notion of *transaction flows*. Since political systems operate both internally and externally through communications, these communications can be assessed in terms of interchanges of physical things or of information. Such transactions can include trade, transportation patterns, migration, tourism, student exchanges, first class mail, telephone and telegraph traffic, movies, and the like. One of the most useful means of measuring these transactions is through construction of an Index of Relative Acceptance, or RA index. This is a measurement of the percentage by which the amount of transactions, for example, in terms of exports, between

---

[17] CIA judgments about the initial strength of the Viet Cong were dismissed, indications from computer war gaming in 1964 that massive bombing of North Vietnam would strengthen the Communists were disregarded, and President Johnson began large-scale bombing of the North in March 1965. *Newsweek*, July 5, 1971, p. 21.

Former Secretary of State Dean Rusk has acknowledged that he and other decision-makers erred in underestimating the endurance and will power of the North Vietnamese. Source: interview on NBC television, July 2, 1971.

two countries is either greater or less than "the hypothetical amount that would be proportional to the overall share of each of these two countries in the total flow of transactions among all countries in the world."[18] The virtue of this RA index lies in its ability to indicate mutual preference or avoidance in transactions between two countries or among groups of countries. Because the figure is a positive or negative proportion, it is far more stable and less subject to sharp year-to-year fluctuation than any kind of calculation based on absolute figures would be. The value of such broad-gauged indices—and several of them are used together—is to provide an indication of major trends in transactions and mutual responsiveness. But beyond this, international politics is characterized fundamentally by relations across national boundaries. These relations largely take the form of transactions, and the significant point is that such transactions can be analyzed, measured and mapped. We are thus not concerned with trade ratios and mail flows as factors in themselves—indeed alone their value is trivial—but only as they provide evidence of international relations in their most fundamental sense.[19]

The application of certain of these concepts and analytic techniques to contemporary Western Europe may provide further clarification of the cybernetic logic. Thus an examination of the record of political and economic integration between France and West Germany during the 1950s and 1960s reveals relationships that are

---

[18] Karl W. Deutsch, Lewis J. Edinger, Roy C. Macridis and Richard L. Merritt, *France, Germany and the Western Alliance: A Study of Elite Attitudes on European Integration and World Politics* (New York: Scribner's, 1967), p. 220. For a more detailed discussion see Bruce M. Russett, *Community and Contention: Britain and America in the Twentieth Century* (Cambridge, Massachusetts: M.I.T. Press, 1963), pp. 33–36; also Karl W. Deutsch and I. Richard Savage, "A Statistical Model of the Gross Analysis of Transaction Flows," *Econometrica* 28 (July 1960): 551–72.

[19] Considerable literature exists on the possible manipulations of transactions data. On salience and covariance, see Karl Deutsch in Philip E. Jacob and James V. Toscano, eds., *The Integration of Political Communities* (Philadelphia: Lippincott, 1964), pp. 51–53; on mail flows, see Deutsch, ibid., pp. 75–82; on telephone traffic and content analysis, see Deutsch, ibid., pp. 82–84; on trade matrices and RA indices, see Russett, *Community and Contention*, p. 35, and *International Regions and the International System* (Chicago, Rand McNally, 1967), pp. 149–52; see also James V. Toscano in Jacob and Toscano, *The Integration of Political Communities*, pp. 100–110, Deutsch and Savage, "A Statistical Model," and Deutsch, "Toward an Inventory of Basic Trends and Patterns in Comparative and International Politics," *American Political Science Review* 54 (March 1960): 46–47.

predictable through the cybernetic approach.[20] Integration between two or more countries creates a diplomatic decision system. When the capabilities of this system are greater than its loads the system functions effectively in the direction of its goal of further integration; in this case the establishment of European unity. When the decision system becomes overloaded, system performance falters. In the Franco-German case, diplomatic decision making functioned effectively in the early 1950s, was then interrupted during 1954–56 (the period of the French rejection of the European Defense Community), resumed its progress during 1957–62, was disrupted once again during 1963–65 (the period of the de Gaulle veto of Britain's Common Market application, controversy over participation in the United States' proposal for a European multilateral nuclear force, and disputes about decision making in the EEC), and then appeared to revive in the late 1960s. The overall pattern is one in which there is a direct relationship between low points in progress toward the institutionalization of integration and a high degree of diplomatic stress. Diplomatic decision making functioned effectively toward the goal of European unity in periods when there were high capabilities for pursuing integration and relatively lower loads upon decision making systems. Interruptions in the construction of regional integration occurred in the face of overloads upon the European diplomatic decision system. Since system overload—in cybernetic terms—is measured by the ratio of capabilities to loads, rather than by absolute amounts of either, it is instructive that the regional and international strains that caused the breakdown of 1963–65 were more numerous and severe than the issues of the 1954–56 period. Because of the solid advancement in European system capabilities, as measured by transaction ratios and the growth of governmental and non-governmental institutions along regional lines, in the early sixties it took a demonstrably greater load to bring the movement toward European integration to a halt than it had a decade previously.[21]

More broadly, the Western European lesson appears to indicate the importance of high and positive transaction flows as a necessary precondition for political and economic integration. While a "common-sense" observation may lead to the conclusion that France and

---

[20] See Donald Puchala, "Patterns in West European Integration," *Journal of Common Market Studies* 9 (December 1970): 137.
[21] Ibid., p. 139.

Germany have always had, as European neighbors, a great deal to do with each other, the *evidence* of transaction flows indicates otherwise. The data instead reveal that during the 1920s and 1930s France and Germany actually had significantly less to do with each other on a proportionate basis than with other countries of the world. In cybernetic terms, the RA indices of international transaction flows between these two countries, as measured for trade, mail, travel and student exchanges, were almost consistently negative.[22] It was only after World War II that the gross transaction flows began to shift in a positive direction.

Another study utilizing the cybernetic approach also provides evidence that contradicts a widely held impressionistic viewpoint about international politics. In this case, a study by Bruce Russett [23] dealing with the relationships between Britain and the United States has shown that contrary to the idea that the experience of mutual support and alliance in two world wars has brought closer ties between the two countries, the reverse actually occurred. That is, based on indices provided by trade figures, student exchanges, mail flows, and telephone and telegraph traffic, Russett has established that Britain and the United States are actually less responsive to one another than they once were.

The application of the communications approach to integration has already been treated in chapter three, but some additional points are here in order. Specifically, because transactions are the basis for mutual responsiveness among states, and because cybernetics assumes that a high mutual relevance encourages cooperation, the analysis of transactions makes possible a very useful measure of integration.[24] Correspondingly, attention to the balance between loads and capabilities provides further analytic benefits. These techniques also provide the basis for assessing how well-integrated a country may be internally. Deutsch in particular has placed great stress on the research question of whether communications boundaries coincide with or cut across political boundaries, for when these boundaries are not coincident it is predictable that the political ones

---

[22] Puchala's data are summarized in Deutsch, Edinger, et al., *France, Germany and the Western Alliance*, pp. 224–27.

[23] *Community and Contention.*

[24] Technically, it is assumed that there is also mutual covariance of rewards (i.e., what is good for one side is also beneficial for the other). See Karl W. Deutsch and J. David Singer, "Multipolar Power Systems and International Stability," *World Politics* 16 (April 1964): 390–406.

will be resisted, with disruptive implications.[25] What is more, the transactions data also reveal, contrary to common-sense notions, that (in an age of modern air travel and new means of international communication) countries are becoming not more interdependent but less so. As measured by foreign trade as a percentage of national income and by the proportion of GNP going through the governmental sector, the cybernetic approach finds that countries are actually more self-preoccupied than ever, and that this closure tends to increase with size.[26]

IV. Transactions, Communications, and International Relations

What impact has the communications approach had upon international relations theory in general? Sharply differing assessments have been made. On the one hand a critic finds cybernetics unhelpful and "inherently inappropriate." [27] This criticism stems from the judgment that a theory of international relations based on cybernetics and feedback is only a metaphor. The difficulty is said to be that while in the engineering field cybernetics has produced important and formalized propositions for predicting the quality of system adaptation, the application of cybernetics to international relations fails to produce similar advantages. This is the case because not all international relations fits within the cybernetic framework. Instead it only does so under a special set of circumstances by which, first, the behavior of any actor is repetitive and variable; second, the distance of a system from its goal is affected by the system's own behavior; and third, the goal itself relates to some environmental trait.[28] More fundamentally, the same argument rests on the contention that it is unhelpful to treat international relations in cybernetic terms because international relations itself is not a system.

These criticisms are profound and yet they rest on definitional

---

25 Deutsch, "The Impact of Communications Upon International Relations Theory," in Abdul A. Said, ed., *Theory of International Relations: The Crisis of Relevance* (Englewood Cliffs, N.J.: Prentice-Hall, 1968), p. 76.
26 Deutsch, *Nerves of Government*, p. x.
27 Bobrow, "Transition from International Communications," p. 1.
28 Ibid., p. 26.

criteria, which may be of limited relevance. The question of whether international relations itself does or does not constitute a "system" is treated in chapter six (Systems Theory), but it is appropriate to note here that a negative answer to this question would not necessarily compromise the validity of the communications approach. Thus to dwell upon the point as a test of the utility of cybernetics is unrewarding. This is so because cybernetics itself stands or falls less as a *general* theory of international relations, i.e., a set of interrelated propositions that cover the field as a whole, than as a *partial* theory, or a framework applicable only to limited portions of the field.[29] As noted in the introduction to this chapter, it resembles game theory in this respect. If we treat cybernetics not as a full theory, but as a means of viewing complex systems, it may still possess considerable utility.[30] And even when the criticism of the cybernetic approach rests on the assumption that not all international relations fits within its bounds, but only that portion to which the above three criteria apply, the applicability of cybernetics remains. For there is little in the descriptions of system and human behavior in terms of the cybernetic model to imply that those kinds of international relations phenomena falling outside it need to be forced into a framework they do not fit.

Apart from this set of criticisms, however, other important criteria do exist for assessing the virtues and limits of the communications approach. First, there is the question of whether indices based on transaction flows do or do not provide a valid tool. Some objections here can be more readily dismissed than others, as, for example, is the case with those that focus upon a particular index (e.g., mail flow) and belabor it as crude or simplistic. It has already been observed that such arguments lose force because they misunderstand the application of transaction flow data. The indices, when properly utilized, constitute no more than part of a broader whole. Several sets of measurements must be taken together, and the ensemble is an aid or supplement—not a substitute—for analysis and judgment. While the criticism has also been made that such gross quantitative

---

[29] On general versus partial theory, see Stanley H. Hoffmann, "International Relations as a Discipline," in Hoffmann, ed., *Contemporary Theory in International Relations* (Englewood Cliffs, N.J.: Prentice-Hall, 1960), pp. 9–10.
[30] See, for example, Roger W. Cobb and Charles Elder, *International Community: A Regional and Global Study* (New York: Holt, 1970), pp. 7–8. It is true, however, that Burton's book is subtitled, "A General Theory."

indices seem, for example, to treat every letter as equal—whether a communication between two heads of government or two taxi drivers—it must be kept in mind that communication patterns among political elites are treated separately, for example by content analysis of the elite press or by elite opinion surveys.[31] A more apt criticism of transactions indices concerns how they are to be weighted. That is, are trade ratios, mail flows, student exchanges, survey data, and amount of attention in the elite press all of equal importance or are some (e.g., trade) far more important than others (e.g., mail)? The problem becomes evident on the occasions when various indices exhibit conflicting positive and negative values. One can acknowledge the major contribution of the transactions data as objective evidence in the study of otherwise emotional and highly subjective topics such as nationalism and sovereignty and yet be aware of this limitation. In the absence of a more precise weighting, only broad-gauged judgments can be made.

For example, if between France and Germany all indices move together in a positive direction, there is clear evidence of increasing mutual responsiveness conducive to integration. Yet what conclusions are to be drawn when the indices move in different directions? Thus Karl Deutsch, focusing on certain kinds of transaction flows, has identified a halting in the process of Western European integration since the mid-1950s.[32] Deutsch and his coworkers relied on five different strains of evidence: elite interviews, mass opinion polls, a survey of arms control proposals, content analysis of newspapers and periodicals, and a large body of aggregate data about actual behavior (trade, student exchanges, travel, migration, mail). However another researcher, Ronald Inglehart, dealing with the same problem, has reached a virtually opposite conclusion: that European integration may have begun to make real progress only since the late 1950s.[33] The reason for this difference is that Inglehart's conclusions rest on data concerning attitudes among the younger generation in Western Europe. He also challenges Deutsch's use of transaction flows on the basis that absolute increases in intra-European trade, tourism, and student exchanges are more important

---

[31] See Russett, *Community and Contention*, pp. 37–39.

[32] Karl W. Deutsch, "Integration and Arms Control in the European Political Environment: A Summary Report," *American Political Science Review* 60 (June 1966): 354–65.

[33] Ronald Inglehart, "An End to European Integration?" *American Political Science Review* 61 (March 1967): 91–105.

than a stagnation in their ratios.[34] Such different conclusions are inevitable as long as the matter of the weighting and usage of indices remains unresolved or imprecise.

Another unresolved problem concerns the significance of transaction flows as *cause* or *effect* of integration.[35] Specifically, does a high and positive pattern of transaction flows between two countries in some way facilitate integration, or does it merely provide evidence confirming that integration has taken or is taking place? If the former holds, then transaction flows are critical as a cause or precondition of integration; if the latter relationship applies, then transactions are a useful noncausative measurement (just as a high reading on a thermometer provides information on but does not cause the hot weather it measures).

Donald Puchala's cautious treatment of transactions leans toward the causative side. While he finds that they are neither necessary nor sufficient preconditions for integration, and that the most one can conclude from the Western European case is that changes in international communication preceded movement to regional political merger, he does assert that the shift in transaction flows to mutual relevance, attentiveness and responsiveness was a necessary part of the *European* integration process, and the sequence of integration in the region can be summarized as "transactions, institutions, polity formation and then legitimacy or support."[36] Deutsch and Russett deal with this fundamental question by finding that both cause and effect may be involved. Thus one formulation attributed to Deutsch is that "cohesiveness among individuals and among communities of individuals can be measured by—and is probably promoted by— the extent of mutual relationship or interaction among them."[37] Similarly Russett asserts that transactions contribute to the development of community and are also promoted by the existence of com-

---

[34] Still other research dealing with the same problem reaches conclusions that are based on data involving the construction of governmental and non-governmental institutions established along cross-national lines. See Puchala, "Patterns in West European Integration."

[35] Hedley Bull raises this point in his anti-behavioral article, "International Theory: The Case for a Classical Approach," *World Politics* 18 (April 1966): 373–75. Ernst Haas has also criticized the communications approach on this basis.

[36] "Patterns in West European Integration," pp. 139–40.

[37] Cited by Philip Jacob and Henry Teune, in Jacob and Toscano, *The Integration of Political Communities*, p. 23.

munity.[38] While this formulation remains somewhat vague, it is true that a process of mutual reinforcement is not illogical. After all, the concept of positive feedback does in fact depict a reinforcing or cyclical process. Understood in these terms there is some logic in the description of transactions as both cause and effect of integration. In sum, the relationship of transaction flows to integration is almost certainly a highly complex one of both cause and effect and is not entirely resolved. The implication is that while these indices are highly useful, they must be employed with considerable care and sophistication and with awareness of their limitations.

What then of the virtues of the communications model? John Burton has suggested that its widespread adoption as a means of looking at the world by analysts and policy-makers can have significantly beneficial results. Whereas the various models or approaches that concentrate on some aspect of power suggest no outcome to international conflict short of recurrent warfare or disaster, the communications model makes more conspicuous the existence of goal-changing options for decision-makers. The relevance of Burton's argument rests on his contention that the political scientist, in revealing the behavior forced upon decision-makers, can make them more aware of alternatives apart from the obvious fatalistic ones inherent in the power politics approaches. It may be that Burton overstates the virtuous consequences of any shift to the communications approach from a more traditional international relations framework. And his perspective has been challenged on the grounds that it is by no means self-evident that international affairs will suddenly be conducted on the basis of peace and mutual respect once statesmen accept this changed perspective. Thus, for example, there is nothing in cybernetic theory to dictate whether international behavior will be either violent or peaceful when the feedback process itself is either good or bad.[39] Yet the real contribution of cybernetics, with its shift in emphasis from power or drives to steering is probabilistic rather than absolute. It betrays a lack of subtlety in judgment to require that in order to be justified any proposed innovation must be capable of bringing about a Manichean reversal of practice. Rather, the adoption of this different framework may be regarded as

---

[38] *Community and Contention,* p. 33.
[39] Bobrow, "Transition from International Communications," p. 27. In fact, the cybernetic approach does allow for the possibility of self-closure and pathological learning. Deutsch, *Nerves of Government,* p. xii.

beneficial because it is in some way conducive to improved inter-national outcomes. By providing for increased scrutiny of the adversary's decision process and perception of alternatives, the com-munications approach displaces existing emphases on ideas of power, prestige, and commitment that have a propensity to present others as inferior and irresolute or as omniscient and insatiable. For the power perspective can lead to such injudicious prescriptions as that outlined by the then Secretary of State, Dean Rusk, in a July 1965 memorandum:

The central objective of the United States in South Vietnam must be to insure that North Vietnam not succeed in taking over or determining the future of South Vietnam by force.

We must accomplish this objective without a general war *if possible.* . . . The integrity of the U.S. commitment is the principal pillar of peace throughout the world. *If that commitment becomes unreliable, the Communist world would certainly draw conclusions that would lead to our ruin and almost certainly to a catastrophic war.*[40]

Conceivably, adoption of the communications approach would bring with it more careful consideration of "Communist world" (Russian? Chinese? North Vietnamese? Cuban?) calculations and in all likeli-hood would produce judgments no less informed that those of the former Secretary of State. The value of this approach is that at a minimum it opens *possibilities* that traditional or power approaches may rule out and thus creates not a certainty but at least a propensity toward more judicious judgments and the consideration of other-wise neglected alternatives.

While Deutsch's application of a steering perspective based on cybernetic concepts may not develop all the power of the original engineering theory, it does provide a coherent conceptual scheme, and not a mere analogy, for building theories and models for com-munication and control in international relations. In its difference of orientation from more traditional frameworks it is likely to affect our own perspectives, the questions we ask, the data we seek, and ultimately the conclusions we draw about the nature of international politics.

---

[40] Quoted in U.S. Defense Department study of the Vietnam war, the Pentagon Papers, as reported by the *Washington Post* and cited in the *New York Times,* June 20, 1971, p. 27. Italics added.

From a distinctly normative standpoint the cybernetic approach also possesses some valued characteristics. Its emphasis is on openness rather than closure, the preservation of communications possibilities with a "potentially inexhaustible environment and a potentially infinite future," and the rejection as pathological of frameworks that make survival and self-respect difficult. As Deutsch aptly observes:

. . . we must either accept intellectual impotence and probable defeat, or we must trust in irrationality, blind luck, and "muddling" through. . . , or else we must increase substantially our powers of thought and perception in terms of our ability to feel for others and to act competently and effectively to help them. We must increase, therefore, the capacities of our intellectual equipment by a substantial amount. . . .[41]

And cybernetics derives its likely utility from its capacity to aid in this enterprise.

Indeed, it may even be that the theoretical study of international relations will come into sharp conflict with prevailing political and foreign policy orthodoxies. As Burton has put it, though with a certain degree of overstatement, the challenge to existing ideas and practices in the foreign policy realm is as drastic as that of Keynesianism to the economic orthodoxies of the 1930s. At that time, reversal of accepted economic policy was a prerequisite for economic stability; now, an analogous reversal is required if we are to hope to attain the goals of peace and security.[42]

Meaningful for f.p. Prescriptive

BIBLIOGRAPHY

ASHBY, W. ROSS. *An Introduction to Cybernetics.* New York: John Wiley, 1956. A sophisticated and partly mathematical introduction to cybernetics for biological and social scientists.

BURTON, JOHN W. *International Relations: A General Theory.* New York and London: Cambridge University Press, 1965. Burton finds that the role of force and power has decreased since 1945 and that orthodox power theory is now an inadequate and undesirable basis for dealing with international relations. We should instead employ concepts and

[41] Deutsch, *Nerves of Government,* p. xvi.
[42] See Burton, *International Relations,* p. 273.

models that concentrate on the decision-making process in terms of steering, communication, and feedback.

CHASE, P.E. "Feedback Control Theory and Arms Races," in *General Systems: Yearbook of the Society for General Systems Research,* Vol. XIV, 1969, edited by Ludwick Von Bertalanffy, Anatol Rapoport and Richard L. Meier. Ann Arbor: Society for General Systems Research, 1969. A mathematically sophisticated treatment of arms races in terms of feedback processes.

DEUTSCH, KARL W. *The Nerves of Government: Models of Political Communication and Control.* New York: The Free Press, 1966. The basic statement of the cybernetic approach as applied to politics.

DEUTSCH, KARL W., and RICHARD I. SAVAGE. "A Statistical Model of the Gross Analysis of Transaction Flows," *Econometrica* 28 (July 1960): 551–72. Sets out the details for computing the index of relative acceptance.

RUSSETT, BRUCE M. *Community and Contention: Britain and America in the Twentieth Century.* Cambridge, Mass.: M.I.T. Press, 1963. Measures trends in Anglo-American mutual responsiveness, partly in terms of international political communication. Examines patterns of transaction flows and elite communication.

WIENER, NORBERT. *Cybernetics: Control and Communication in the Animal and the Machine.* Cambridge, Mass.: M.I.T. Press, 1948. The original delineation of cybernetics as applicable to machines, institutions and individuals.

———. *The Human Use of Human Beings: Cybernetics and Society.* Boston: Houghton Mifflin, 1950. Provides a treatment of cybernetics more accessible to the non-scientist.

5

International

Power

and

Conflict

Speculation about the nature of power and the causes of conflict has extended as far back in time as any aspect of international relations. The components and uses of national power have been the subject of endless inquiry and analysis, as have the determinants of war. But the development and proliferation of nuclear weapons have lent new urgency to these questions. Explanations and hypotheses about war are numerous and contradictory. We have been told that war is a universal human trait or that wars are carefully planned by decision-makers, that wars are the result of impersonal historical forces or the consequences of the ambitions of individual national leaders, that violence inheres in the nation-state or that violence results from errors of judgment on the part of decision-makers.[1] And the analysis of international conflict is by no means confined to a small coterie of political scientists. On the one hand, Sigmund Freud, the father of psychoanalysis, lamented the nature of man, which he viewed as likely to make the abolition of war impossible. On the other hand, an American president has ventured the judgment that with the ending of the Vietnam War, "I seriously doubt if we will ever have another war. This is probably the very last one."[2]

---

[1] See, for example, Dean G. Pruitt and Richard C. Snyder, eds., *Theory and Research on the Causes of War* (Englewood Cliffs, N.J.: Prentice-Hall, 1969), p. xi.

[2] Richard M. Nixon, interviewed by C.L. Sulzberger, *New York Times*, March 10, 1971.

The causes of international conflict surely constitute the primordial question in the study of international politics; thus the ability of contemporary theory to come to grips with the subject constitutes a fundamental test of its possibilities and limitations. This chapter will first explore the definition and measurement of international power, then turn to an analysis of why conflict occurs and what the major possibilities of conflict resolution may be.

I. The Measurement of Power

Power has long been regarded as central to both the understanding and the practice of world politics. Traditional theorists from Machiavelli on have regarded power as both an end in itself and as a means to such varying national objectives as security, peace, aggrandizement, prosperity, and justice.[3] According to one of the most well known formulations of the power concept, its content and use depend on a wide range of political and cultural factors, so that power covers all social relationships that establish the control of man over man, ranging from outright violence to subtle psychological ties.[4] And national decision-makers have long been obsessed with questions of power, whether expressed as Stalin's derisive and myopic comment, "How many divisions has the Pope?" or more subtly, in terms of judging if a Southeast Asian country possesses the will and ability to defend itself.

Any serious analysis of international politics must deal with national power as a prelude to arriving at conclusions about conflict, but power has seldom been measured in a systematic or reliable manner. Yet if the actual conceptualization and measurement of power is difficult, it is not impossible. For example, social science has been able to accomplish the measurement of human phenomena as complex and as subtle as intelligence, so the possibility of gauging the concept of power certainly cannot be ruled out on an a priori basis. And the likelihood of attaining a reliable measurement or index of such complicated phenomena is facilitated by the fact that

---

[3] Vernon Van Dyke, *International Politics* (New York: Appleton-Century Crofts, 1957), p. 175.

[4] Hans J. Morgenthau, *Politics Among Nations: The Struggle for Power and Peace,* 3d ed. (New York: Knopf, 1960), p. 9.

what matters is not whether a given index or test really measures intelligence or power but how well it predicts behavior.[5]

The basic requirement is for an *operational definition* of power. That is, measurement requires a procedure precise enough so that any researcher employing the same definition will obtain identical results. The importance of this replicability is enhanced by the fact that theoretical statements or propositions that involve such abstract concepts are not directly verifiable but are instead tested in terms of their operational definitions. There is, as the late H. V. Wiseman observed, no logical way to prove that a given operational definition actually does tap the underlying theoretical concept. The validity of it is substantially a matter of "argued plausibility and consensus of opinion." [6]

Thus before seeking a measurement of power it is first necessary to grapple with the problem of definition. A great deal depends on what exactly is to be measured and how it is defined. For example, Hans Morgenthau has contended that what sets politics apart as an autonomous sphere of action and understanding separate from economics or ethics or religion is the concept of interest defined in terms of power.[7] Yet types and definitions of power abound and many of them describe different things. Morgenthau found power to be the very essence of international politics, yet he has been criticized for the imprecision of his power concept, which in different contexts implied that power was a major goal of policy, a motive of political action, a relationship, and a means to an end.[8] Indeed, one survey of power as a concept has found seventeen different definitions.[9] In a sense, this definitional ambiguity may be likened to the fable of the blind men and the elephant. In this well

---

[5] This point is made by Michael Nicholson, in *Political Studies* 17 (March 1969): 138.

[6] H. V. Wiseman, *Politics: The Master Science* (London: Routledge & Kegan Paul, 1969), p. 41.

[7] Morgenthau, *Politics Among Nations*, p. 5. Power has been a central concept for a number of other important and serious theorists. See, especially, Inis L. Claude, Jr., *Power and International Relations* (New York: Random House, 1962), and E. H. Carr, *The Twenty Years' Crisis, 1919–1939*, 2d ed. (London: Macmillan, 1949).

[8] See K. J. Holsti, "The Concept of Power in the Study of International Relations," *Background* 7 (1964): 179–94.

[9] A finding by Dennis G. Sullivan, cited in Norman Z. Alcock and Alan G. Newcombe, "The Perception of National Power," *Journal of Conflict Resolution* 14 (September 1970): 335.

known—and perhaps overworked—tale, several blind men encounter an elephant but touch different parts of it. One bumps into a leg and believes he has encountered a tree; another likens the end of a tusk to the point of a sword; and another touches the tail and thinks it is a snake. They are all describing portions of the elephant, but their absence of vision prevents any comprehensive description, let alone correct identification of the object as an elephant.

Deutsch has provided a categorization of power that can serve as a point of departure for the problem of definition.[10] The first and most commonly conceived type of power involves brute force, or the capacity to prevail over resistance. Here it is a question of direct tests of strength, of hardness and rigidity, or of pecking orders. But the political efficacy of this type of power may be severely constrained, so that massive thermonuclear capability, which falls within this category, does not automatically convey the ability to persuade the voters of Chile to support a pro-United States presidential candidate, nor to win over the "hearts and minds" of a Southeast Asian population—as the United States belatedly discovered at a substantial cost in Vietnam. This dilemma of ineffective power is by no means confined to the United States. The experience of the Soviet Union in Eastern Europe reflects an unstable equilibrium in which Rumania, Czechoslovakia, and, to a lesser extent, Hungary and Poland threaten to drift away from the Soviet orbit because the sheer weight of Russian power, while effective in the short run, has not sufficed to bring about a lasting shift in national attitudes.

This first kind of power does lend itself to measurement in probabilistic terms. Deutsch finds that gross power can be regarded as the probability that a system would be able to impose a specified amount of change upon its environment; and net power is definable as the difference between this imposed change and the cost of change to the system. Applied, for example, to Vietnam, such a measurement would indicate that the United States' net power there was limited because any effort to overwhelm the North Vietnamese and Viet Cong could only have been achieved through an immense and unacceptable cost to the United States.

The limitations of this first kind of power lead to concern with a second type: the power to achieve precise results. The latter is as

---

[10] See Karl W. Deutsch, *The Nerves of Government: Models of Political Communication and Control* (New York: The Free Press, 1966), pp. 110 ff.

different from the former as the skill to thread a needle is from the force of a charging elephant. What counts is not the power of nuclear weapons systems, but the ability to attain desirable foreign policy outcomes. The essentials here are precision, steering, and control, precisely the elements that comprise successful cybernetic systems; and the efficiency of such systems is measurable in terms of feedback.[11]

A third type of power has been defined by Robert Dahl; it is the ability to shift the probability of outcomes, and this conceptualization provides the opportunity for at least a crude quantification of power.[12] Taking care to acknowledge that a causal relationship cannot necessarily be inferred from a statistical association, Dahl employs a probability statement to represent the power of an actor. This power is defined as equal to the difference in the probability of an event given some action by the actor, and the probability of an event given no such action.[13]

The use of this procedure may be illustrated with an example of group influence in British politics.[14] The National Farmers' Union (NFU) sought to have the government exclude agriculture from a proposed European Free Trade Area during 1956–58. Under these circumstances, the probability of the government's actually doing so was perhaps 0.9, while the probability had the NFU not made such an appeal was 0.3. Thus the NFU's power, in terms of the ability to shift the probability of outcomes, was 0.9 minus 0.3, or 0.6. Although the figures cannot be regarded as precise, they do reflect relative orders of magnitude and are thus of substantial heuristic value.[15] A calculation of NFU power as in the order of 0.6

---

[11] See chapter four, above, on Cybernetics.

[12] Robert Dahl, "The Concept of Power," *Behavioral Science* 2 (1957): 201–15. Aspects of Dahl's formulation have been criticized by Duncan MacRae and H.D. Price, "Scale Positions and 'Power' in the Senate," *Behavioral Science* 4 (1959): 212–18; and by Peter Bachrach and Morton S. Baratz, "Two Faces of Power," *American Political Science Review* 56 (1962): 947–52.

[13] "The power of an actor, A, would seem to be adequately defined by the measure M which is the difference in the probability of an event, given certain action by A, and the probability of the event given no such action by A." Dahl, "The Concept of Power," p. 214.

[14] This example is drawn from Robert J. Lieber, *British Politics and European Unity* (Berkeley: University of California Press, 1970), pp. 288–89.

[15] In defense of pinning numbers on ordered categories in a "wisely arbitrary" fashion, see Edward Tuftee, "Improving Data Analysis in Political Science," *World Politics* 21 (July 1969): 644–46.

is an index of very considerable influence. (By contrast, a figure of 0.0 would have reflected a state of total powerlessness, a figure of 1.0 would have represented absolute determination of the outcome.) Related calculations can also be made for successive periods so that during 1961 the influence of the NFU in obtaining certain agricultural safeguards as part of Britain's Common Market negotiating position can be determined as about 0.4. Subsequently, during the time of the 1966–67 Labour Government application the NFU's influence fell to around 0.1. Based on these calculations we have a measure of the decline in agricultural influence during three stages of European policy making, from 0.6 to 0.4 to 0.1. These figures provide a certain measure of evidence for reaching conclusions about aspects of the British decision-making process.

Fourth, derived from the work of Talcott Parsons, there is the concept of power as a kind of currency in the exchange of social functions. Here power may be conceived of as the currency of the political system in the way that money is the currency of the economy. That is, we cannot eat or dress or shelter ourselves with money, but money permits access to the goods and services with which we can be fed, clothed and housed. And just as the flows of currency are well suited to quantitative analysis by economists, so too this conception of power should provide the opportunity for quantification. As Deutsch puts it, from the viewpoint of the currency of politics, "power is the coordinated expectation of significantly probable *sanctions,* that is, of substantial shifts in the allocation of highly salient values." [16] This conceptualization of power as a currency extends well beyond mere sanctions and enforcement. Prestige can be understood to bear the same relationship to power as credit does to cash, and physical force the same relation to power as gold to paper money. Thus just as bankers can lend more money than is deposited, so governments commit themselves to enforce more laws than they can at any one time, should massive challenges arise simultaneously. Both functioning economies and viable political systems require a large measure of voluntary compliance and cooperation; without them, neither can function successfully. And, as the late Arnold Wolfers commented, there are still further analogies between money in the market economy and power in international politics. Money can have sharply differing purposes for

---

[16] Deutsch, *The Nerves of Government,* pp. 120–21. Deutsch's discussion of Parsons is illuminating, see pp. 116 ff.

various individuals: it can be regarded as a steppingstone for things valued for their own sake, it can provide freedom of action and economic security, or it can be hoarded by a miser as an end in itself. So too, among nations power is mostly valued as a scarce commodity that provides the basis for satisfying such urgent national needs as security; it can also provide more fortunate nations with security reserves; or the power drive can become inflamed so that it attains the status of a pathological urge.[17]

Beyond setting out several definitions of power it is worthwhile to deal with certain aspects of the measurement of power. Traditionally, factors of economic strength, military resources, population, and territory have been thought to comprise national power. Deutsch has suggested that the dimensions of power be divided into the categories of domain, range, and scope.[18] Domain, signifying over whom or what power is exercised, applies to elements of national power such as population, territory, and gross national product. A focus on domain, in terms of GNP, provides some perspective on international politics and affords explanatory and even predictive possibilities. For instance, in 1950 the United States' GNP accounted for 46.4 percent of the total world GNP, whereas despite huge absolute increases in American production, the United States' relative share in 1970 actually slipped to about 32 percent. This may help to explain why American international political power appears to have declined somewhat over the past decade. In the same span the share of the USSR will have climbed from 9.5 percent (about ⅕ of the United States' figure) to 15.9 percent (or about ½ of the United States' share). Correspondingly, the rise of Japan and West Germany can be identified, along with some decline in the relative standing of Britain and India (see Table 5-1).

As for the category of range, this applies to the difference between the highest reward (e.g., as measured by wealth, GNP, or foreign aid) and the worst punishment (e.g., destruction) that a nation can dispense. Nuclear weapons are most salient in this category, and the five nuclear powers (the United States, USSR, the United Kingdom, France, and China) stand alone in their capacity to inflict massive punishment by means of these weapons. But the

---

[17] Arnold Wolfers, *Discord and Collaboration* (Baltimore: Johns Hopkins Press, 1965), pp. 105–6.
[18] See Karl W. Deutsch, *The Analysis of International Relations* (Englewood Cliffs, N.J.: Prentice-Hall, 1968), pp. 28 ff.

TABLE 5-1

National GNP as Percentage of
World Total in 1950 and 1970

Rank	1950	%	Rank	1970	%
1.	United States	46.4	1.	United States	32.0
2.	USSR	9.5	2.	USSR	15.9
3.	Britain	8.1	3.	Japan	6.1
4.	France	4.2	4.	W. Germany	6.0
5.	W. Germany	3.8	5.	France	4.9
6.	China	3.6	6.	Britain	3.4
7.	Canada	3.3	7.	Italy	2.8
8.	India	3.3	8.	Canada	2.8
9.	Italy	2.1	9.	China	2.6
10.	Japan	2.1	10.	India	1.4

Sources: Bruce Russett, Trends in World Politics (New York: Macmillan, 1965),
p. 121, and New York Times Encyclopedic Almanac 1972, 3rd ed. (New York:
1971).

range of power that nuclear power provides is not readily trans-
ferrable into political power, so that Britain, for example, at the
very time she was developing a nuclear capability has seen her
potential influence steadily diminished. This leads us to a third
category, the scope of power, or the set of behavioral relations effectively subject to it. With the growth of economic management and
the welfare state in the developed Western countries, and of central
economic management in the Communist countries, nations have
steadily increased their power over the daily lives of their own
citizens. Deutsch suggests that measurement of the increasing proportion of GNP that flows through the governmental sphere provides a highly useful index of this expanded scope of power.

From the foregoing discussion it is evident that military force is
by no means the only significant dimension of power. But it is also
the case that inherent in military power there is a certain self-
reversing component. During the postwar decades, for example,
Japan and West Germany have expended a relatively low average
proportion of their GNP on defense (Japan about 1 percent, Germany 5 percent), and have enjoyed impressive increases in economic
growth (and in potential military power). Similarly, Sweden and
Switzerland have spent an average of less than 5 percent per year
and have also exhibited strong growth. By contrast, the United

States, USSR, and United Kingdom have averaged from 8 percent to 11 percent (possibly as high as 14 percent in the case of the Soviets), and have grown at a relatively slower pace. Thus while the United States has until recently maintained an overwhelming nuclear superiority by expending vast sums of money and talent, the American railway and electricity systems have failed to keep pace with contemporary demands, urban areas have suffered from lack of funds, educational expenditures and medical services have not kept abreast of demand, and a host of unmet needs have become increasingly evident.[19] Some of these neglected areas are less important than others, but the constraints on investment in educational, technical, and scientific sectors can only be imposed at the expense of future growth. Investment in basic research reflects a similar pattern. In Germany and Japan less than 15 percent of expenditures for basic research have gone into military and space efforts, whereas in Britain roughly 60 percent of expenditures go into these fields plus atomic energy. The figures for the United States are even higher.[20]

One additional means of measuring power is provided by the rank-size law, which permits prediction of the rank order of a given unit provided its size is known, or else the prediction of size if rank is known. The measurement may pertain to population, GNP, or territorial size. Actually, the principle was first observed in the late nineteenth century by linguists. They had discovered surprising regularities in the relative frequency with which various words occurred in any written text, so that when different words were listed in their order of frequency, the tenth word on the list was found in the text roughly $\frac{1}{10}$ as often as the first, the 100th word $\frac{1}{100}$ as often as the first, and so on. And, not only words, but popu-

---

[19] To cite just one example of an unmet medical need, during 1968 the United States infant mortality rate per 1,000 live births was 22.1. By contrast, the figure for the United Kingdom was 18.7, and for Sweden 12.6 (the world's lowest rate). The United States ranked 23d. See *New York Times*, May 31, 1971, and *Annual Abstract of Statistics* (London: Her Majesty's Stationery Office, 1969), p. 36.

[20] From a 1962 report by Senator Hubert H. Humphrey, cited in Richard J. Barnet and Marcus G. Raskin, *After 20 Years: The Decline of NATO and the Search for a New Policy in Europe* (New York: Vintage, Random House, 1965), p. 68. As of 1963, 52 percent of all engineers and scientists in the United States were employed on projects financed by the defense or space programs. See Bruce M. Russett, *What Price Vigilance? The Burdens of National Defense* (New Haven and London: Yale University Press, 1970), p. 135.

lation rankings and certain other aggregate phenomena have been found to follow the same law.[21] To cite just one example, by taking the population of the world's most populous country, China (730 million), it is possible to estimate the population of the eighth most populous country, Brazil, by using the formula: $nt = K \pm K/2$, where n = rank, K = population of the top country, and t = population of the nth country. The resulting calculations tell us that the estimated Brazilian population is 91 million. Actually, the correct figure is 88 million, so the prediction is a relatively close one.[22] The value of the rank-size law, apart from its novelty, is to facilitate estimation of missing data, which form a part of any calculations about national power.

At this point, we have a number of different definitions and measurements of power. The fact of these differences is not in itself harmful if we consider that markedly different operational definitions of intelligence or of the consumer price index can also exist to provide independent measurements of the abstractions to which they refer. When compared with earlier traditional usages, the various operational definitions of power constitute a definite step in the direction of rigor and precision, but it is also true, as K. J. Holsti notes, that power concepts are not useful for all aspects of the study of international politics. Power, whatever its conceptualization, does not account for the determination of national goals nor for all international relationships, nor all trade relations, nor the increasingly important operations of international functional organizations. Thus, while the power concept retains a major place within the discipline, and can indicate important areas of research and investigation, it cannot function satisfactorily as the theoretical core of international relations.[23] Power does, however, provide a basis

---

[21] For example, "If two cities have ranks j and k, respectively, in the list, their populations will be approximately in the ratio k/j." *The Behavioral and Social Sciences: Outlook and Needs,* published by the National Academy of Sciences and Social Science Research Council (Englewood Cliffs, N.J.: Prentice-Hall, 1969), pp. 71–72.

For the original and more complex treatment of this, see George K. Zipf, *Human Behavior and the Principle of Least Effort* (Cambridge, Mass.: Addison-Wesley, 1949), especially chapter ten.

[22] However, the limits are very broad (plus-or-minus 46 million). Population figures are those of the UN Statistical Office, cited in *New York Times Encyclopedic Almanac,* 1970, p. 362.

[23] Holsti, "The Concept of Power."

for both group and national identity. It is these separate entities, possessing autonomous power, that interact at the international level; and conflict is the most visible aspect of this general interaction.[24] Let us therefore turn to the area of conflict to see whether analytic efforts have proceeded any further in that field of inquiry.

II. Why Does International Conflict Occur? Some Traditional Views and Contemporary Insights

Of all the questions with which the study of international politics must deal, the question of why war occurs is surely the most critical. International politics can and does end the lives of large numbers of people, civilians as well as combatants. While the nuclear stalemate has so far forestalled a World War III, a succession of bloody conventional conflicts has taken place since 1945. The list of recent wars or armed conflicts includes a multitude of cases, and a similar list could easily be compiled for earlier periods. To cite only some of the more celebrated recent examples since 1945, there have been wars involving Indochina, Algeria, China, Korea, Hungary, Nigeria, the Congo, Cuba, Cyprus, the Yemen, India vs. Pakistan, West Pakistan vs. East Pakistan, China vs. India, and Israel vs. the Arab countries (three times).[25]

Diverse explanations for the occurrence of war are almost as numerous as the different wars themselves. There are views that

---

[24] Lewis Coser indicates that conflict can perform an integrative social function. See his illuminating book, *The Functions of Social Conflict* (New York: The Free Press, and London: Collier-Macmillan Ltd., 1956), especially chapters one and nine.

[25] Civil wars are included since the division between this type of conflict and an interstate war is not always clear, particularly once outside countries come to the aid of the combatants (as they usually do), and because the ferocity and casualties in civil wars (e.g., China, Nigeria, Pakistan) are often greater than in "traditional" wars.

J. David Singer and Melvin Small treat ninety-three wars between 1816 and 1965. Among their criteria for inclusion on the list are that the population of each belligerent be over one-half million, and that the best estimate of total battle deaths surpass 1,000. "Alliance Aggregation and the Onset of War," in J. David Singer, ed., *Quantitative International Politics* (New York: The Free Press, 1968), pp. 258–59.

blame all conflict upon the Communists, as for example that of the editor-in-chief of the Hearst Newspapers, William Randolph Hearst Jr.:

Wherever you go, whomever you talk to, the important world problems all have a common denominator: Communism.

The world's troubles would become relatively inconsequential if it were not for the everlasting-conniving and trouble-making of the Reds.[26]

Similar views were once held by Richard Nixon: "If it weren't for the Communist threat, the free world could live in peace," [27] and by Harry S Truman: "There are some people—and I regret to say some governments—who have not yet accepted the fact that but for Russian intransigence the world would now be enjoying the pursuits of peace." [28] On the other hand, the Communists have tended to take the reverse view. The analysis of V.I. Lenin held that international conflict was caused by the dynamics of imperialism, but that Communist states would enjoy harmonious relations of international proletarian solidarity. And from yet another perspective, Woodrow Wilson found the cause of war to reside in the absence of self-determination and democratic government in the afflicted parts of the world. In contrast to the above views, the late Bertrand Russell blamed war not upon a given type of political system but upon human weakness, particularly the wickedness and stupidity of statesmen. Still others have focused upon population pressures, economics, rigidifying of the balance of power, individual political ambition, the effects of technological change, various types of imperialism, and the mythical international Zionist conspiracy. Most of these are single-factor explanations, and yet the dimensions of conflict seem far more complex than any one factor can account for. For example, the major combatants on both sides at the outbreak of World War I (France, Russia and Britain vs. Germany and Austria-Hungary) where not opposed along Communist vs. non-Communist or democratic vs. nondemocratic lines, but instead were mostly non-revolutionary constitutional monarchies, which had in common their

---

[26] *San Francisco Sunday Examiner and Chronicle,* December 22, 1968.
[27] *New York Times,* November 19, 1953, quoted in Kenneth N. Waltz, *Man, The State and War* (New York: Columbia University Press, 1959, p. 157.
[28] *New York Times,* April 28, 1957, quoted ibid.

private-enterprise economic systems and the Christian religion. By contrast the key division in the Korean war was on a Communist (North Korea, China) vs. non-Communist (South Korea, United States) basis. Yet there are also many wars based on entirely different factors such as religion and territory (Israel vs. the Arabs, India vs. Pakistan), colonialism (France in Algeria; Portugal in Angola, Mozambique, and Portugese Guinea), and ethnicity or tribalism (Hausas vs. Ibos in Nigeria; West Pakistan vs. East Pakistan).

Given this plethora of explanation, as well as the diversity of historical experience, how can we best make sense of the phenomenon of war? The problem is not merely to choose among a host of contradictory theories at diverse conceptual levels, but also to determine whether a social scientific theory is even worthwhile here. That is, it has been asserted that theory is impractical, that generalizations about the causes of war may be impossible, and that the theoretical exercise is fruitless since war is in any case inevitable.[29] But, if the subject is approached in probabilistic instead of absolute terms, and significant individual factors rather than single causes are sought, theorizing about the nature of war is entirely feasible.

The most useful point of departure for an analysis of conflict is provided by Kenneth Waltz. In his book, *Man, The State and War,* Waltz identifies three divergent "images," or sets of explanations, for the occurrence of war. The first image finds in man himself the locus of important causes of war. The second image concentrates upon the nature of individual states, and the third finds the cause of war to lie not in men or states but in the nature of the nation-state system itself. Historically, most explanations for the causes of war, and for its mitigation or prevention, have fallen into one of these three images.

The first-image explanations rest upon the assumption that the causes of war are to be found in the nature and behavior of man. Thus the philosopher Spinoza explained violence by reference to human imperfections, whereby passion displaced reason. He held that, out of self-interest, men ought to cooperate but instead they engage in deadly quarrels. And John Milton found war to be inevitable because men were irrevocably evil. The viewpoint of Bertrand Russell also fits into this category since it places the blame

---

[29] Pruitt and Snyder deal with these criticisms, *Theory and Research,* pp. 3–5.

upon the shortcomings of decision-makers. More broadly, Russell asserted that just as children run and shout from impulse and dogs bay at the moon, so grown men quarrel, boast, beat at each other, and murder.[30]

As Waltz notes, both optimists and pessimists are subsumed under the first image. The pessimists find the real nature of man to be essentially flawed and beyond correction, so that little can be done to prevent the recurrence of war. The optimists characterize man as basically or potentially good and society as essentially harmonious provided that certain prescriptions are followed so that mankind will be uplifted or enlightened. Psychological conflict theories also fit into this category. Studies that concentrate upon the emotional makeup of decision-makers, as well as more broadly based psychological approaches, are undertaken on the assumption that the root cause of international conflict lies in the nature of man. Some psychological analyses have assumed that because war represents aggressive behavior by nations, an understanding of its causes can be obtained by examining the determinants of aggressive behavior in individuals. They have therefore stressed, and perhaps over-emphasized, the importance of aggression. For example, a president of the American Psychological Association has proposed the development of a drug that national leaders could take in order to decrease their emotional propensities to react to some future international crisis by starting a nuclear war; he has also suggested that this "psychological disarmament" might even be negotiated among nations much in the way that military disarmament has been the subject of contemporary negotiations.[31] However, Herbert Kelman notes that the conclusion of most psychologists and other social scientists has been that psychological and anthropological research results do not provide support for the assumption that war is rooted in human nature and is thus inevitable. Efforts to determine the causes of war that proceed from individual psychology rather than analysis of relations between nations are, according to Kelman, of dubious relevance. Psychology does have contributions to make, for example, from work on the psychology of aggression, the motivations of decision-makers, and the distortion of perception under con-

---

[30] Bertrand Russell, *Why Men Fight* (New York: Century, 1916), p. 8, cited in Donald A. Wells, *The War Myth* (New York: Pegasus, 1967), pp. 177–78.
[31] Address by Dr. Kenneth B. Clark to the annual meeting of the American Psychological Association, and interview as reported in the *New York Times*, September 5, 1971.

ditions of stress, but there cannot be a self-contained psychological theory of international relations as an alternative to economic or political theories. Instead, there must be a more general international relations theory to which psychological analysis can make a substantial contribution once the relevant points at which it is appropriate are identified.[32]

First-image approaches (i.e., those which concentrate upon the individual) fall well short of providing any comprehensive explanation for why war occurs. Man seems to possess substantial capacities for both cooperation and conflict, so analysis must proceed to the state and systemic levels within which drives are channeled. The analyses of international conflict that fall within the second-image category operate on the assumption that war depends on the type of national government or the character of a national society. One implication of this perspective is that while human nature may not be changeable, social and political institutions are. The theoretical perspectives of Lenin and Woodrow Wilson surely fit within this category, but neither withstands the test of experience. Thus Lenin held that because of the dynamics of imperialism, capitalist states promoted war, whereas the relations of Communist states would be peaceful. But this analysis, together with the earlier prediction of Friedrich Engels that "Between a Socialist France and a ditto Germany an Alsace-Lorraine problem has no existence at all," [33] is belied by the experience that the Baltic countries, Hungary, Czechoslovakia and China have had with the USSR. Thus there is clear evidence that Communist states are not markedly more peaceful in their international conflict behavior. And Woodrow Wilson's perspective that democracies are more peaceful, while it is authoritarian and monarchical states that are aggressive, fares little better than Lenin's when one regards the encounters of Mexico, Spain, Cuba, and the countries of Indochina in their international experiences with the United States. More comprehensively, Evan Luard's study of warfare in the modern world during the century from 1865 to 1965 finds little evidence that any particular kind of government (whether authoritarian or liberal, Communist or democratic, mili-

---

[32] Herbert C. Kelman, ed. *International Behavior: A Social-Psychological Analysis* (New York: Holt, Rinehart and Winston, 1966), pp. 5–7.
[33] Engels to Bebel, October 24, 1891, in Marx and Engels, *Selected Correspondence,* tran. Torr, p. 491, quoted in Waltz, *Man, The State and War,* p. 121.

tary or civilian) is more prone to undertake armed attack than any other kind.[34]

A number of other philosophical or historical analyses have also sought to link the type of nation to the occurrence of international conflict. In the nineteenth century, for example, Auguste Comte and Herbert Spencer characterized military conquests as typical of the behavior of backward agrarian societies, whereas they believed industrial countries exhibited more peaceful international behavior because a stable international system provided conditions more conducive to the increasing of their wealth through economic production.[35] But L. F. Richardson (the late British scholar noted for his mathematical models of arms races) demonstrated that these views were not supported by historical evidence. Thus while wars had greatly increased in their destructiveness since 1820 (the start of the industrial revolution in Britain), their frequency per unit of time did not significantly decline. There was therefore no confirmation of the theory that industrialized countries were less prone to engage in warfare. On the basis of a more recent quantitative study, however, there is some evidence that rural international systems are more peaceful than transitional industrial international systems.[36] In other words, the stresses of industrialization seem to be positively correlated with higher levels of war than are to be found in areas that have either not yet industrialized or have already completed the process of industrialization.

An important large-scale effort to arrive at systematic conclusions regarding the relationships between a nation's attributes and the likelihood of its involvement in international conflict has been undertaken by R. J. Rummel and a group of scholars.[37] Utilizing data on 230 variables, including thirteen separate measurements of foreign conflict behavior (e.g., severance of diplomatic relations, ambassadors expelled, threats, military action, mobilization, wars, nationals killed in foreign violence), the study tested eleven dif-

---

[34] Evan Luard, *Conflict and Peace in the Modern International System* (Boston: Little, Brown, 1968), p. 66.

[35] Michael Haas, "Social Change and National Aggressiveness, 1900–1960," in Singer, *Quantitative International Politics*, p. 216.

[36] Ibid., pp. 216 and 244.

[37] Rudolph J. Rummel, "The Relationship Between National Attributes and Foreign Conflict Behavior," in Singer, *Quantitative International Politics*, pp. 187–214.

ferent hypotheses. Individual hypotheses related foreign conflict behavior to level of economic development, extent of international communication, amount of international cooperation, totalitarianism of a government, national power, instability, military capabilities, psychological motivations of a people, national values, number of geographic borders, and combinations of some of these characteristics. The results of this hypothesis testing produced overwhelming empirical evidence that there are no common domestic and foreign conflict behavior dimensions. In other words, little relationship exists between the above characteristics and national involvement in foreign conflict. Rummel does caution, however, that all these conclusions must be regarded as tentative until additional studies have been completed.[38]

Another systematic study relating domestic to foreign conflict behavior has produced findings somewhat contradictory to those above. Jonathan Wilkenfeld has discovered that there are some positive relationships between these two kinds of behavior if one controls for type of nation, type of conflict, and time lags. However, Wilkenfeld acknowledges that the generally small size of the correlation coefficients indicates that not very much of the variance in foreign conflict behavior can be explained on the basis of the domestic dimension.[39] In effect, the degree of contradiction in the results of the two systematic studies is less important than the fact that both of them provide evidence that second-image explanations of the causes of war are extremely weak because there is either little (Wilkenfeld) or no (Rummel) relationship between the type of nation and the incidence of international conflict.

For a more promising approach to the causes of war we must therefore turn to the third image, or the level of the international system. The essence of the third image is that the ultimate cause of warfare inheres in the very condition of the international system, which Waltz and many others have identified as one of international anarchy. That is, states exist in an international milieu that lacks

---

[38] Rudulph J. Rummel, "Dimensions of Foreign and Domestic Conflict Behavior: A Review of Empirical Findings," in Pruitt and Snyder, *Theory and Research*, pp. 225–26. The sole exception to this lack of relationship was the number of geographic borders that a nation shared with others, but even here Rummel found the evidence ambiguous.

[39] Jonathan Wilkenfeld, "Some Further Findings Regarding the Domestic and Foreign Conflict Behavior of Nations," *Journal of Peace Research*, No. 2 (1969): p. 155.

any effective means for the peaceful resolution of conflicts because of the absence of any accepted overall authority or sense of community. Unlike the position of individuals within an ordered nation-state, the security and interests of nations are not by-and-large protected by some established authority with a monopoly of the means of violence nor by a judicial system for the authoritative resolution of disputes; instead, individual nations exist in an environment where each is dependent for its security almost wholly upon its own efforts, and where the ultimate means of conflict resolution or settlement of disputes is one of power, coercion, or force. This perspective upon the nature of the international system reflects the basic orientation of contemporary international relations analysis. A summary of this outlook has been offered by George Modelski and it is worth quoting at length:

States (or nations, or countries) are political systems possessing
community, consensus, and a monopoly of the means of violence;
by contrast international systems lack these characteristics. Hence
the basic difference between domestic and international politics is
most strikingly manifested in the fact that while peace is the rule in
domestic politics, war is the distinguishing feature of international
relations. The state of war is the direct result and the unavoidable
consequence of the lack of community, consensus, and monopoly of the
means of violence in the world at large. Thus war, the expectation of
war, and the diplomatic and strategic behavior consequent upon it
become the *explicanda* of international relations.[40]

The formulation of this view extends at least as far back as Thomas Hobbes, who contrasted the existence of civil society at the national level with the state of nature at the international level. For Hobbes, individuals in a state of nature fear for their own safety and each is driven to attack others for fear that the others might injure him. Finding life in this condition "solitary, poor, nasty, brutish, and short," men turn to civil society, or the state, for the security on a collective basis that they lack individually. A paradigm for the predicament of man in the state of nature, and by implication for nations in the international environment, was offered by Jean Jacques Rousseau in his story of the stag:

---

[40] George Modelski, "The Promise of Geocentric Politics," *World Politics* 22 (July 1970): 617.

Assume that five men who have acquired a rudimentary ability to speak and to understand each other happen to come together at a time when all of them suffer from hunger. The hunger of each will be satisfied by the fifth part of a stag, so they "agree" to cooperate in a project to trap one. But also the hunger of any one of them will be satisfied by a hare, so, as a hare comes within reach, one of them grabs it. The defector obtains the means of satisfying his hunger but in doing so permits the stag to escape. His immediate interest prevails over consideration for his fellows.[41]

The implications of this story are that self-interest may make cooperation impossible even when all parties have an interest in the enterprise, and the same conditions may also make war inevitable even though none may wish it.

Comparisons of this international state of nature with a domestic state of nature vary markedly. Hobbes' state of nature for nations is, according to Stanley Hoffmann, better than it is for individuals. While both conditions are characterized by insecurity, conflict, deficiency of law, a quest for power, and the need to be armed and ready, the international condition is the more bearable because the states provide a cushion for individuals. States are stronger than men and therefore have less fear of annihilation. The existence of the state gives security to citizens, and even the existence of an international war does not affect all men.[42] Roger Masters, while criticizing Waltz's stress on the probability of war as an underestimation of the elements of legality and order in international politics, has likened international relations to a primitive political system without a government, in that both have no formal governmental structures to judge and punish, require reliance on self-help and violence, produce law only from custom and bargaining (or retaliation and deterrence) rather than legislation, and have political units with multiple functions.[43] But the international form of "ordered anarchy" has, according to Masters, two major differences that make it actually worse than a primitive political system: first, whereas primitive political culture is typically homogeneous and conducive

---

[41] From Rousseau's *Inequality,* cited in Waltz, *Man, The State and War,* pp. 167–68.

[42] Stanley H. Hoffmann, *The State of War: Essays on the Theory and Practice of International Politics* (New York: Praeger, 1965), pp. 60–61.

[43] Roger Masters, "World Politics as a Primitive Political System," *World Politics* 16 (July 1964): 597–609.

to stability, the international system exhibits radically different political cultures and technological differences; second, where the primitive system is conducive to the limitation of change, the international one tends toward far greater instability, which may bring on chaos.[44]

This image of the international system may provide an effective explanatory perspective upon important kinds of international behavior. System-generated conflict can occur regardless of the intentions and interests of individual states, and system behavior may even differ sharply from that of its components. In game theory the case of Prisoner's Dilemma (treated in chapter two) is an effective theoretical instance of this problem, and arms races are another example.

The position of Israel in the Middle Eastern conflict provides apt illustration of behavior compelled by system constraints. Since Israel's inception as a state in 1948, its overriding concern has been to exist within its own borders. But for its very existence, Israel has not been able to rely upon any external international body or individual nation, and several vivid examples have provided evidence that this is no tenuous theoretical judgment. In November 1947, the United Nations voted to partition the British Mandate over Palestine into Arab and Jewish national states. Upon the expiration of the British Mandate in May 1948, the response of the surrounding Arab countries was to launch a military effort to obliterate the Israeli part. In this instance the Israelis were compelled to fight for their survival largely unaided, and the role of the UN was restricted to effecting an eventual ceasefire. After eight years of tension and growing hostilities, a crisis resulted in the 1956 Suez expedition, which left Israel momentarily in possession of the Sinai Peninsula and the Gaza strip. Israel withdrew in 1957 on the basis of a guarantee from the United States, Britain, and France that her ships would have freedom of navigation through the international waterway of the Straits of Tiran.[45] But in May 1967, President Nasser demanded the removal of UN forces from Sharm el Sheik. The immediate compliance of U Thant with this request provided a

---

44 Ibid., pp. 613–15.
45 From 1956 to 1959, Israeli goods were allowed to pass through the Suez Canal in ships not flying the Israeli flag. But in 1959, Egypt blockaded this route by detaining a number of ships and seizing their cargoes. See Keesing's Research Report, *The Arab-Israeli Conflict* (New York: Scribner's, 1968), p. 8.

glaring example of the reality of the international state of nature problem as far as Israel was concerned. That is, the weak embodiment of international community in the United Nations proved quite unable to assert itself as any kind of arbiter between the two main parties: Egypt and Israel. Similarly, Nasser's announcement that he was closing the Straits of Tiran not only evoked no effective response from the international community (despite a clear violation of international law, which created a *casus belli*) but also revealed that the pledges made by the United States, the United Kingdom, and France would not or could not be implemented.

At this point the Israeli predicament reflected the reality of Rousseau's vision that no authoritative international arbiter exists with the means of imposing order. Existing international guarantees had been vitiated, Egyptian armor had poured into the Sinai, and speeches of Arab leaders promised to drive the Israelis into the sea. Israeli decision-makers were then faced with two possible choices: to do nothing in the hopes that the Arabs would not in fact attack (or that if they did attack, the international community would not acquiesce in the destruction of Israel), or to seek to preserve Israel's own security by a preemptive strike. In a sense, the nature of the international system compelled what in game theory would be termed a mini-max strategy: the choice of the second alternative. For if the worst possible outcome were to take place after Israel had elected the first option, a sudden Arab onslaught might well have succeeded in decimating the Israelis, who had little room for tactical retreat and maneuver on dry land. But if the Israelis chose to preempt, they would in effect play it safe. At worst they would fight a (possibly unnecessary) war from an initially favorable position and possibly stand to occupy additional territory as a buffer. Given the facts that the Israelis had no room for retreat or mistake, that to wait for an absolute certainty that the Arabs would actually attack might conceivably have meant the slaughter of their entire population, and that the international system provided absolutely no means of security upon which Israel could rely, the Israelis thus had a strong inducement to launch the preemptive attack that began the Six Day War.

In the ensuing years Israel has faced the same international dilemma, but in a less acute form. Her choices are whether to take risks in seeking a peace that the international community has shown itself wholly unable to enforce, or to maintain an endless (or incipient) state of hostilities against the numerically superior Arabs as the price of relying upon herself for security. The third image provides the perspective that there is no obvious solution to this dilemma. In the absence of a UN strong enough to impose a settlement, end the regional arms race, and guarantee the borders in an effective and inalterable manner, there can be little prospect of peace in the Middle East.

The Arab-Israeli conflict is only one case among many that demonstrate the problem of the international system. Evan Luard's study of war indicates that since 1945 most wars have arisen not out of deliberate policies of aggrandizement or aggression but from specific incidents and disputes.[46] This type of conflict would be particularly susceptible to effective resolution in a more ordered international environment, but in the absence of such a framework, international dynamics propel the parties in the direction of war. War thus occurs not so much because of desires or disputes, but because of the absence of anything that could curb them. As Waltz observes, the immediate (or efficient) causes of war may lie to some extent in the nature of men and of states, but the permissive cause is to be found in the third image: the inability of the international system to prevent war. The conclusion is that war is a necessary consequence of the nation-state system.

III. Conflict and Peace: The Possibilities of War Prevention

Apart from the general third-image explanation, there is clearly no single specific cause of war and therefore no single way to achieve the prevention of war. As long as a nation-state system exists there will be international conflict leading to war. The most profound solutions involve some means of altering the international system so as to end the situation of independent nation-states existing in an environment where no authoritative arbiter of disputes exists. The commonly mentioned requirement here is the establishment of an international civil society in the form of a world government, federation, or other more limited international body with effective jurisdiction and powers. With the existence of this kind of arrangement, conflicts such as that over Alsace-Lorraine (a factor in three wars between France

---

[46] Luard, *Conflict and Peace*, p. 316.

and Germany), or the South American territorial disputes leading to the Paraguayan War of 1864–70 (in which 90 percent of the Paraguayan male population was killed) would presumably have been as susceptible to peaceful resolution as the contention between the states of California and Arizona over Colorado River water rights was within the United States during the 1960s.

Bertrand Russell warned that mankind must establish a world state within a very few decades, or no later than the year 2000, or else face annihilation. And, because of the existence of thermo-nuclear weapons, the pressing importance of this ideal type of solution should not be minimized. But the record of the past several centuries of international politics has been that individual nation-states fiercely resist the derogation of their own political sovereignty. More limited technical or functional bodies have been created to exercise jurisdictions formerly those of the states, and the League of Nations and United Nations have represented small but significant steps in the direction of some kind of international "civil society." Nonetheless, both the structure and experience of the United Nations have reflected ultimate national retention of sovereignty, particularly on the part of the more powerful states. While the creation and proliferation of nuclear weapons have made the need for an inter-national solution a matter of overwhelming importance, this has not precipitated any marked increase in the willingness of nation-states to entertain a significant diminution of their own powers. Thus if the twin perils of international anarchy and nuclear holo-caust have not so far sufficed to bring about any significant steps toward some variant of the ideal solution, what other alternatives are there?

To begin with, there may in fact be no solution at all, and we cannot rule out the possibility that the international system will collapse into an utterly catastrophic nuclear war with the potential for destroying civilized life. On a lengthy time perspective, several generations or a century at most, there is a strong and logical probability that the choice is indeed between some form of inter-national government and some variant of a nuclear Armageddon. In the short run, however, the range of possibilities is far wider. Raymond Aron has observed that apart from the twin choices held out by Bertrand Russell there is a third path of quasi-regulation of inter-state violence, or peace through fear. And in fact a condition of nuclear deterrence has characterized world politics in the atomic age and is likely to do so for some time. Deterrence theories posit the now familiar balance of terror that has so far ensured a certain stability in Great Power relationships, forestalling any nuclear war, though not by any means preventing large non-nuclear wars. In addition, deterrence theory has had the effect of calling to our attention the surprisingly complex range of possibilities that exist between peace and all-out nuclear war. Herman Kahn, for example, has offered a scenario with an elaborate forty-four step "escalation ladder," with seven thresholds (disagreement, don't rock the boat, nuclear war is unthinkable, no nuclear use, central sanctuary, central war, city targeting) and seven stages (subcrisis maneuvering traditional crises, bizarre crises, exemplary central attacks, military central wars, and civilian central wars). (See Table 5-2.)

TABLE 5-2

An Escalation Ladder

A Generalized (or Abstract) Scenario

Aftermaths

Civilian Central Wars
- 44. Spasm or Insensate War
- 43. Some Other Kinds of Controlled General War
- 42. Civilian Devastation Attack
- 41. Augmented Disarming Attack
- 40. Countervalue Salvo
- 39. Slow-Motion Countercity War

(City Targeting Threshold)

Military Central Wars
- 38. Unmodified Counterforce Attack
- 37. Counterforce-with-Avoidance Attack
- 36. Constrained Disarming Attack
- 35. Constrained Force-Reduction Salvo
- 34. Slow-Motion Counterforce War
- 33. Slow-Motion Counter-"Property" War
- 32. Formal Declaration of "General" War

(Central War Threshold)

Exemplary Central Attacks
- 31. Reciprocal Reprisals
- 30. Complete Evacuation (Approximately 95 percent)
- 29. Exemplary Attacks on Population
- 28. Exemplary Attacks Against Property
- 27. Exemplary Attack on Military
- 26. Demonstration Attack on Zone of Interior

Table 5-2 (Continued)

(Central Sanctuary Threshold)

Bizarre
Crises
{
25. Evacuation (Approximately 70 percent)
24. Unusual, Provocative, and Significant Countermeasures
23. Local Nuclear War—Military
22. Declaration of Limited Nuclear War
21. Local Nuclear War—Exemplary

(No Nuclear Use Threshold)

Intense
Crises
{
20. "Peaceful" World-Wide Embargo or Blockade
19. "Justifiable" Counterforce Attack
18. Spectacular Show or Demonstration of Force
17. Limited Evacuation (Approximately 20 percent)
16. Nuclear "Ultimatums"
15. Barely Nuclear War
14. Declaration of Limited Conventional War
13. Large Compound Escalation
12. Large Conventional War (or Actions)
11. Super-Ready Status
10. Provocative Breaking Off of Diplomatic Relations

(Nuclear War Is Unthinkable Threshold)

Traditional
Crises
{
9. Dramatic Military Confrontations
8. Harassing Acts of Violence
7. "Legal" Harassment—Retortions
6. Significant Mobilization
5. Show of Force
4. Hardening of Positions—Confrontation of Wills

(Don't Rock the Boat Threshold)

Subcrisis
Maneuvering
{
3. Solemn and Formal Declarations
2. Political, Economic, and Diplomatic Gestures
1. Ostensible Crisis

Disagreement—Cold War

Source: Herman Kahn, On Escalation: Metaphors and Scenarios (New York: Praeger, 1965), p. 39.

If Kahn's scenario is too fanciful, we do have the empirical evidence of a generation of world politics in a nuclear setting, with experiences ranging from the Cuban Missile Crisis to the Nuclear Non-Proliferation Treaty, and from the increasing economic and political integration of Western Europe to the near-genocidal slaughter in East Pakistan. In the short run, the nature of international politics, in terms of both cooperation and conflict, has not been simplified.

Given these considerations, what possibilities may there be for the limitation of war? In more traditional terms, Evan Luard has urged us to concentrate upon the level of the nation-state, arguing that effective change at either the individual human level or the international systemic level is impossible in the short run. Luard advises that we seek peace by the laborious and uncertain method of reforming national behavior and procedures. Although disarmament or world government would be more desirable, neither alternative is probable. We must therefore seek to achieve increased international toleration, greater play for the force of world opinion, and increased consensus among governments.[47] This is not far different from what Deutsch has urged in terms of seeking a cooperative rather than a competitive model of international politics, and by arguing that if national governments can be made to visualize more carefully the payoffs of their various courses of action, to increase their reality-testing capabilities,[48] and to avoid closure, then it need not be inherent for them to think and operate in terms of power and conflict.

But the problem of conflict mitigation can also be approached on a systemic level. Deutsch and Singer have explored the dynamics of system-generated stability on the basis of increased multipolarity. They find that in terms of decreased frequency and intensity of warfare, a multipolar international system may be more stable than a bipolar one. Their conclusion rests on two premises: first, that a multipolar system results in a substantial increase in interactional opportunity, which also has the effect of lessening the amount of attention that national actors can devote to one another; and second, that in the short run this will result in less severe international conflict because some minimum percentage of a nation's external

---

[47] Luard, *Conflict and Peace,* pp. 312–15.
[48] See Karl Deutsch and Dieter Senghas, "Toward a Theory of War and Peace," paper presented at the 65th Annual Meeting of the American Political Science Association, New York, September 2–6, 1969. The authors argue that the chances for peace are improved by spreading efforts for peace over all systemic levels, ranging from the individual through small groups, parties, and nation states, to the international system level.

attention must be directed toward another nation before it can adopt behavior tending toward armed conflict. Thus in a rigid bipolar system only one interactional relationship, in terms of a dyad or pair, is possible and the two actors will have 100 percent of their external attention available to devote toward each other. However, the existence of three major nations results in three possible pairs, four nations produce six pairs, etc.[49] By the time five nations are involved there are ten possible pairs, and nations now have an average of only 10 percent of their external attention available for interactional opportunity with any one other actor. Based partly on signal-to-noise ratios in cybernetics, and partly on arbitrary estimation, Deutsch and Singer observe that it may be possible to assume it unlikely that any country "could be provoked very far into an escalating conflict with less than 10 percent of the foreign policy attention of its government devoted to the matter."[50]

The Deutsch and Singer model actually rests on a more subtle basis than might appear from the above analysis. Elsewhere, Deutsch has stressed the importance of the relationship between frequency of interaction and covariance of rewards. Four types of relationships can be conceived of based on the possibility that frequency of interaction can be either high or low, and covariance of rewards can be either positive (meaning what is beneficial for one side is also beneficial for the other) or negative (meaning the reverse).[51] If two nations have a high frequency of interaction and positive covariance of rewards, then their relations are likely to be characterized by integration or a high degree of amity. But if they have the same high frequency of interaction and a low covariance of rewards (in other words a situation of considerable contact but opposed interests) then they are likely to find themselves in conflict. When nations have a low frequency of interaction and positive covariance of rewards, then relations will be friendly or correct, and when a low frequency and low covariance, then cool or distant. This

---

[49] Karl W. Deutsch and J. David Singer, "Multipolar Systems and International Stability," *World Politics* 16 (April 1964): 394. Their formula for possible pairs is $N(N-1)/2$.

[50] Ibid., p. 399.

[51] Waltz discusses an analogous four-fold model of Kurt Singer's in Stephen L. Spiegel and Kenneth Waltz, eds. *Conflict in World Politics* (Cambridge, Mass.: Winthrop, 1971), pp. 458 ff.

theoretical categorization suggests that conflict is a product of the coincidence of high interaction and the presence of conflicting interests. There are thus potentially two ways to move away from the conflict situation: by shifting to a relationship of high co-variance of rewards (as France and Germany have succeeded in doing via the European Coal and Steel Community and the European Economic Community), or to decrease the frequency of interaction. The Deutsch and Singer approach suggests that the latter alternative is operational in the case of multipolarity.

The virtues of multipolarity in lessening the frequency and intensity of war have not gone unchallenged. Kenneth Waltz has argued that it is actually bipolarity that is the more conducive to international stability, largely because the two powers are prone to conduct themselves more cautiously and responsibly in such circumstances.[52] But Waltz's approach is not based on a systematic study, in contrast to Singer and Small, who find that, in a study of some ninety-three wars in the period from 1816 to 1965, there is a strong positive correlation between a greater number of alliance commitments and more war, and a positive though somewhat lower correlation between system bipolarity and more war.[53] More generally, Singer and Small find that the nature of international relations may have changed over time, so that in the nineteenth century the existence of alliance aggregation and bipolarity predict away from war whereas in the twentieth century they predict toward it. The empirical evidence thus indicates that war in the twentieth century is in fact associated with bipolarity, though it should be recognized that one cannot necessarily impute causality from the existence of statistical correlation. In any event, there is tentative vindication of the Deutsch and Singer position that a shift to a multipolar world will help to increase short-run international stability by decreasing the risk of rapid escalation. There is also an implied policy preference for the encouragement of alliance fragmentation and other efforts at multipolarity. But even here, Deutsch and Singer do not disregard the profound long-range international problem; they acknowledge the long-run instability of multipolar systems and the intractability of the nuclear problem in such a situation, though

---

[52] "The Stability of a Bipolar World," *Daedalus* 93 (Summer 1964): 892–907.
[53] Singer and Small, "Alliance Aggregation and the Onset of War," pp. 282–83.

noting that even in the long run the instability of tight bipolar systems is greater than that of the multipolar type.[54]

IV. Conclusion

Waltz has contended that short of the achievement of effective international integration (the ideal of Kant) or complete isolation of nations (a prescription of Rousseau) —both of which imply the abolition of international relations—conflict will remain inevitable.[55] If this is the case, can systematic studies of conflict and warfare be expected to make contributions that go beyond a remote theoretical understanding? For example, it has been argued that a study such as Singer's, which systematically examines war over the past 150 years, may have little direct relevance in terms of application to future conflict. The nuclear issue here is regarded as particularly intractable, for even a generalized formula derived from a larger body of empirical data might be beside the point when it comes to preventing a cataclysmic nuclear war that, as a single event, might or might not be predictable, but that would foreclose the international future of many nations. The argument has a certain validity, but one that hardly

---

[54] Deutsch and Singer, "Multipolar Systems and International Stability," p. 406.

Still another perspective is offered by Richard Rosecrance. He criticizes the kind of bipolarity described by Waltz (its zero-sum competition and periodic crises enhance the likelihood of war; it employs contradictory definitions concerning the possibilities of change within the system; and it confuses bipolarity with detente), but he also finds flaws in multipolarity (higher probabilities of increased international conflicts, though with reduced intensity; great risks if nuclear proliferation occurs; and the creation of increased uncertainties, which make accidental war more likely). Rosecrance's answer is to set out the traits of a "bimultipolar" system that would combine the most attractive features of both bi- and multipolarity. His system would exhibit sufficient bipolar control of multipolar areas so as to prevent or limit extremes of conflict. In the presence of continued bipolar competition, the two major powers would act to regulate conflict in external areas, but multipolar states would provide a degree of buffering in conflicts between the bipolar powers. Conflict would not be eliminated, but it might be more limited. See "Bipolarity, Multipolarity, and the Future," *Journal of Conflict Resolution* 10 (September, 1966): 314–27, reprinted in James N. Rosenau, ed., *International Politics and Foreign Policy* (New York: The Free Press, 1969), pp. 325–35.

[55] Spiegel and Waltz, *Conflict in World Politics*, p. 474.

eliminates the need or importance of systematic approaches to the problem of war. For one thing, the high incidence of limited war since 1945 indicates that despite the nuclear specter, war has continued as a prominent feature of international politics. In this sense, if systematic analysis can produce a better understanding and prediction of warfare, it may hold out the prospect of an increased ability to prevent or to limit these wars. And an improved understanding of warfare could even be applicable to the overriding nuclear problem, both in terms of limiting lesser wars (from which there is an ever-present danger that a nuclear war might erupt), and in terms of affecting the behavioral and conflict aspects that can persist among decision-makers and countries involved in a prospective nuclear confrontation.

The reality that the one comprehensive solution to international conflict, in terms of the establishment of a world state that would effectively end international politics as we think of it, is not attainable in the foreseeable future should not cause us to assume that nothing fruitful can be accomplished. If we regard the problem of war in probabilistic terms, progress toward its amelioration is feasible. Pruitt and Snyder have observed that because certain features of war can be demonstrated to follow laws of probability we should not regard war as a "mysterious and unalterable affliction." Instead, there is an analogy with airplane accidents, whose frequency also exhibits statistical regularities.[56] Just as we have been able to discover some of the causes of these accidents and thereby reduce (though certainly not eliminate) the problem of airplane crashes, so there may be similar opportunities with regard to the possible application of knowledge about warfare.

There is, of course, not only the problem of obtaining valid evidence and constructing reliable theories about the causes and prevention of war, but also the task of applying such information in a practical way. There can be no certainty that any such knowledge will be utilized, but that order of problem does not even arise unless systematic and verifiable knowledge exists. The immediate task of international political analysis is therefore to develop and refine its own competence and thereby to hold out at least the opportunity of reducing the incidence and severity of warfare.

---

[56] Pruitt and Snyder, *Theory and Research*, p. 218.

BIBLIOGRAPHY

ALLISON, GRAHAM T. *Essence of Decision: Explaining the Cuban Missile Crisis.* Boston: Little, Brown, 1971. A treatment of three implicit conceptual models (rational actor, organizational process, and bureaucratic politics) that can shape the ways in which analysts and decision-makers think about foreign and military policy.

HOFFMANN, STANLEY. *The State of War: Essays on the Theory and Practice of International Politics.* New York: Praeger, 1965. An important collection of Hoffmann's philosophical essays on war and the international system.

KAHN, HERMAN. *On Escalation: Metaphors and Scenarios.* New York: Praeger, 1965. Idiosyncratic and sometimes bizarre speculation on the dynamics of nuclear escalation.

KELMAN, HERBERT C., ed. *International Behavior: A Social-Psychological Analysis.* New York: Holt, Rinehart and Winston, 1966. A collection of original contributions on international behavior, including cross-national perceptions, bargaining and decision making.

LUARD, EVAN. *Conflict and Peace in the Modern International System.* Boston: Little, Brown, 1968. An introductory but sophisticated treatment with emphasis on problems of war and peace.

PRUITT, DEAN G., and SNYDER, RICHARD C., eds. *Theory and Research on the Causes of War.* Englewood Cliffs, N.J.: Prentice-Hall, Inc., 1969. An outstanding volume of systematic work on the causes of war.

RAPOPORT, ANATOL. *The Big Two: Soviet-American Perceptions of Foreign Policy.* New York: Pegasus, 1971. A critical treatment of the perceptions and interactions between American and Russian policy makers and strategists.

STAGNER, ROSS. *Psychological Aspects of International Conflict.* Belmont, California: Brooks/Cole and Wadsworth, 1967. An approach to international behavior and conflict, which utilizes psychological concepts and theories.

THUCYDIDES. *History of the Peloponnesian War.* Translated by Rex Warner. Baltimore: Penguin, 1954. A classic chronicle of the War between Athens and Sparta, which broke out in 431 B.C. Records the "moral deterioration of the Greek world at war" and stands as a great work on politics and the nature of warfare.

WALTZ, KENNETH N. *Man, the State and War: A Theoretical Analysis.* New York: Columbia University Press, 1959. Outstanding treatment of theoretical approaches to war, divided into the categories of the individual, the nation-state, and the international system.

WELLS, DONALD A. *The War Myth*. New York: Pegasus, 1967. A scholarly pacifist treatment, which argues that the chief drives toward war stem from "inept, unthinking, and callous statesman and citizens."

WHITE, RALPH K. *Nobody Wanted War: Misperception in Vietnam and Other Wars*. Garden City, New York: Doubleday, 1970. An approach to the Vietnam conflict by a leading social psychologist.

WRIGHT, QUINCY. *A Study of War*, 2d ed. Chicago: University of Chicago Press, 1965. An important early and comprehensive work on the nature and causes of war.

6

Systems

Theory

It would be no exaggeration to say that it is systems approaches that have dominated the field of broad-gauged international relations theory during the past decade. Systems theory has provided a number of significant advances. It has helped to shift the orientation of the study of international relations away from an earlier emphasis on more anarchic facets of world politics to one that provides greater coherence and broader perspective by viewing international relations in terms of a pattern of "global interdependence." It also offers the opportunity to explore novel or previously neglected aspects of the subject, and it has provided a basis for a more generalized and social-scientific approach to a field of study once dominated by research that was either largely impressionistic or else stressed the historical uniqueness of individual cases.[1] At the same time it would not be too extreme to hold that no subject has remained more opaque and inaccessible to nonspecialists during the past ten years. This chapter will seek to provide a measure of perspective on the contributions and abuses with which systems theory has been linked. To do so, it will first deal with general systems theory, the foundation upon which the various international systems edifices are built, and then turn to an appraisal of international systems approaches in principle and in practice. Finally, the chapter will offer an appraisal of the virtues and weaknesses of the systems theory enterprise.

---

[1] See George Modelski, "The Promise of Geocentric Politics," *World Politics* 22 (July 1970): 629–30.

SYSTEMS THEORY / 121

I. General Systems Theory

General systems theory is a subtle and highly sophisticated construct that originated in the natural sciences in reaction to a prevailing tendency toward rigid compartmentalization of knowledge and an emphasis on narrowly detailed studies. In an effort to stimulate attention toward more general theoretical considerations, as well as to promote the integration of knowledge from other disciplines, general systems theory postulates that a series of abstract systems exists to which all knowledge can in principle be reduced.[2] It defines the concept of the *system* as a set of elements or units, which interact in some way and are set off from their environment by some kind of boundaries. Whether systems are mechanical, organic, human, or social, general systems theory holds that they possess inherent features that are common to all of them. Hence it is helpful to study features of systems generally before seeking to understand any given system individually.[3] Partisans of general systems theory claim that it constitutes the very "skeleton of science" in that it offers a conceptual framework upon which can be hung "the flesh and blood of particular disciplines and particular subject matters in an orderly and coherent corpus of knowledge."[4]

---

[2] See Oran R. Young, *Systems of Political Science* (Englewood Cliffs, N.J.: Prentice-Hall, 1968), p. 14, and Michael Banks, "Systems Analysis and the Study of Regions," *International Studies Quarterly* 13 (December 1969): 347.

[3] John Burton, *Systems, States, Diplomacy and Rules* (Cambridge, England: Cambridge University Press, 1968), p. 5. It should also be noted that definitions of a "system" are numerous and overlapping. E.g., "Any system is a structure that is perceived by its observers to have elements in interaction or relationships and some identifiable boundaries that separate it from its environment." Charles A. McClelland, *Theory and the International System* (New York: Macmillan, 1966), p. 20. And "A system . . . is a set of variables so related, in contradistinction to its environment, that describable behavioral regularities characterize the internal relationships of the variables to each other and the external relationships of the set of individual variables to combinations of external variables." Morton Kaplan, *System and Process in International Politics* (New York: Wiley, 1957), p. 4. Also, "A system is a set of things related in some way so that changing or removing any one thing in the set will make a difference to other things in the system." D. R. Strickland, L. L. Wade R. E. Johnson, *A Primer of Political Analysis* (Chicago: Markham, 1968), p. 7.

[4] Kenneth Boulding, "General Systems Theory: The Skeleton of Science," in *General Systems* 1 (1956): 17, quoted in Burton, *Systems, States, Diplomacy and Rules*, p. 21.

Different General systems theory is sometimes confused with *systems analysis*, but the two terms designate rather different enterprises. Systems analysis is more familiar and understandable; it constitutes a type of methodology that can be considered as no more than the formalized version of clear thinking about complicated problems, whereby these are divided into sections so that each may be concentrated upon individually before the whole is reassembled mentally. If particular portions of the problem cannot be comprehended, they may be "black-boxed," or set aside; or the researcher may confine his study to one subsystem or level, while not losing track of the system as a whole.[5] In other words, systems analysis is really a set of techniques for systematic analysis that facilitates the organizing of data, but which possesses no ideal theoretical goal. By contrast, general systems theory subsumes an integrated set of concepts, hypotheses, and propositions, which (theoretically) are widely applicable across the spectrum of human knowledge.[6]

Some basic propositions within general systems theory are regarded as particularly relevant for use in political science. Oran Young has provided a classification of three broad groups of general systems theory concepts. The first group of these relates to the definition of a system as a whole. Here a system may be relatively open or closed, in terms of the amount of interaction with its environment. Living systems are a kind of open system in a steady state. On a system-wide level, an entity may also be centralized or decentralized, depending on the closeness of the relationships among its components parts. For example, because of the very great looseness within it, the international political system may be said to exist in a highly decentralized state. Perhaps the most important systemic concept is that of *isomorphism*, or the "one-to-one correspondence between objects in different systems which preserves the relationship between the objects."[7] The concept is of particular utility in interdisciplinary studies and the identification of functional correspondences in the principles and processes of systems.

A second category of general systems concepts concerns those concepts that apply to system regulation and maintenance. One of the most important ideas here is that of system equilibrium, which

---

[5] Banks, "Systems Analysis," pp. 346–47.

[6] Young, *Systems of Political Science,* p. 19.

[7] A. Hall and R. Fagen, "Definitions of a System," *General Systems* 1 (1956): p. 18, quoted in Young, *Systems of Political Science,* p. 17.

may be stable or unstable. In open systems, stable equilibrium is termed *homeostasis,* or the ability of a system to maintain its internal balances even while undergoing processes of change.[8] In addition there is the concept of integration, which applies to the principles of organization and to the institutions holding the system together,[9] and the concept of pattern maintenance, which includes system repair and the cybernetic ideas of feedback, learning, and steering.

Finally, there are those system concepts that describe tendencies to growth or decay. The concepts of entropy and its negative are applicable here. Entropy concerns the tendency of all organized systems to run down, or move from a state of greater organization to one of randomness.[10] Negative entropy is the reverse of this process and provides an index of system well-being or durability. Adaptation, or the manner in which a system copes with its environment, is also applicable within the category of concepts related to system growth or decay.

Before attempting to assess the value of general systems theory and then to examine its application in terms of the international political system, it is appropriate to consider several major social-scientific formulations of the general systems approach. One of the most widely known, most important—and least readable—is the construct of Talcott Parsons. Parsons has at various times been regarded as vague, rambling, imprecise, and incoherent.[11] Nevertheless, his work has become central to sociology and, more widely, to social science, so that some comprehension of the Parsonian ap-

---

[8] Young, *Systems of Political Science,* p. 109.

[9] Banks, "Systems Analysis," p. 349. Integration in this systemic sense must be differentiated from its more specific use in terms of national and regional integration, where it denotes relationships of community or cohesiveness among people within a political entity. (See above, chapter three.)

[10] Entropy is discussed at greater length in chapter four of this work.

[11] As Professor W. J. M. Mackenzie has commented, Parsons "disobeys so many of the rules of scholarship which we were taught as students. He writes too much, his definitions are vague; his style is Germanic; he inhabits a great system of an old-fashioned kind; he is continually adding bits on to it; but rarely takes anything away, so that the architecture is ramshackle and subject to puzzling changes and incoherences." *Polititics and Social Science* (Harmondsworth, Middlesex, England: Penguin, 1967), p. 87.

Of Parsons' work, see, e.g., *The Structure of Social Action* (New York: The Free Press, 1949); *The Social System* (New York: The Free Press, 1951); *Structure and Process in Modern Societies* (New York: The Free Press, 1960); and "An Outline of the Social System," in Parsons, et al., eds., *Theories of Society* (New York: The Free Press, 1961).

proach to general systems theory is desirable. The aspects most relevant to the present discussion concern Parsons' view of the essential functions that any social system must fulfill if it is to preserve its own stability and survival. The first of these functions is pattern maintenance, the preservation or reproduction of a system's pattern or essential characteristics. Second, there is the function of adaptation, which pertains to a system's ability to cope with its environment. The third function is goal attainment, or the achieving of whatever goals the system may possess (at a minimum the system will usually have the goal of survival). Fourth, there is integration, which requires that the various parts and functions of the system operate coherently rather than in opposition to each other. By focusing upon these essential functions we can determine a great deal about system behavior and also have a basis for the orderly comparison of systems or of subsystems within a system. Parsons has been criticized for creating no more than an elaborate nonempirical system of matrices and conceptual schemes into which data could be placed. But Karl Deutsch has observed that even the creation of a "good filing system" that assists in systematic ordering and rapid and efficient retrieval of multitudinous data about social and political behavior would be no mean achievement. And he argues that Parsons has done even more than this because an efficient conceptual scheme stresses relevant connections and de-emphasizes less relevant ones. By doing this and by indicating significant variables, it also opens predictive possibilities:

Once a classification scheme or theoretical system is used to highlight particular correlations, the social scientist is already making predictions, at least in probabilistic terms. He is predicting that certain correlations are either critically high or low and that certain relationships will be significantly correlated with others. . . . In this sense what looked like a purely formalistic system turns out to be a system that contains predictive implications when put to actual use.[12]

Thus it can be argued that Parsons has not only created an efficient system for data collection, storage and retrieval, but also one that

[12] Karl Deutsch, "Integration and the Social System: Implications of Functional Analysis," in Philip E. Jacob and James V. Toscano, eds., *The Integration of Political Communities* (Philadelphia: Lippincott, 1964), pp. 180–81.

provides guidelines for relevance and the creation of new knowledge.

Unlike Talcott Parsons' theory, which is delineated from the viewpoint of sociology, the general systems theory of David Easton is constructed from a political science orientation. For one thing, Easton has contributed the important definition of political science as the study of the "authoritative allocation of values" for a society.[13] And Easton also treats the political system as an open system in a steady state, depending on homeostasis to maintain its boundaries and continuing existence within them.[14] The political system is seen as a conversion process, in a continuous interchange with its environment, responding to inputs and producing outputs. Inputs may be either demands upon the system or supports that reinforce its responsive capabilities, and outputs consist of decisions.

Gabriel Almond also discusses the political system in terms of input and output functions. In essence, Almond holds that any political system performs the same input and output functions, but that systems can be compared or differentiated in terms of the structures they possess for performing these functions.[15] Almond labels the major input functions as political socialization, interest articulation, interest aggregation, and political communication. His system output functions include rule making, rule application, and rule adjudication. However, this structural-functional approach tends to be more applicable to comparative politics, in which the various kinds of political systems (democratic, authoritarian, totalitarian)

---

[13] David Easton, *The Political System*, 2d ed. (New York: Knopf, 1971), p. 129. Also see Easton, *A Systems Analysis of Political Life* (New York: Wiley, 1965).

Because it is understood to make these authoritative decisions, the political system is thereby differentiated from other social systems. Cf. the excessively broad definition of Gabriel Almond and G. Bingham Powell, which includes "all interactions which affect the use or threat of use of legitimate physical coercion," and covers governmental institutions and "all structures in their political aspects," such as kinship ties, caste groups, riots, parties, interest groups, and communications media. *Comparative Politics: A Developmental Approach* (Boston: Little, Brown, 1966), p. 18. The Easton definition also seems preferable to those orientations that define political science as the study of power relations (cf. Morgenthau, Lasswell) and are thus too broad in that they fail to distinguish clearly the political realm.

[14] See the lucid discussion by Mackenzie, *Politics and Social Science*, p. 105.

[15] See Ernst B. Haas, *Beyond the Nation-State* (Stanford, California: Stanford University Press, 1964), pp. 59–60.

are compared and contrasted, than to the international political system.

In contrast with earlier traditional and descriptive orientations, general systems theory offers certain advantages. To begin with, it provides major possibilities for organizing and relating otherwise random collections of empirical evidence into a coherent overall framework or system. It redirects attention from strictly formal and legal institutions, such as constitutions, governments, and international organizations, to more broadly defined processes, structures, and entire systems. The criteria of Easton, for example, provide a structured series of questions that can be used to assess the status of an entire system. As John Burton notes, general systems theory makes it possible to break down society into sets of relations that are then susceptible to orderly step-by-step analysis of detail without losing sight of the whole.[16] And Oran Young stresses the analytic value of general systems theory in terms of its provision of widely applicable concepts and models, its potential for standardizing terminology, coding data, and storing information, and its transfer of insights by means of isomorphisms, which also provide important means for exploiting mathematical advances.[17]

But general systems theory also has a number of corresponding limitations. Easton's theory, for example, provides little opportunity to deal with questions of major change or upheaval, and it de-emphasizes questions of power and influence. Young notes that the question of system perspective is not necessarily the most inclusive for political analysis, and that Easton's approach focuses on national political systems more than on the interactions of political systems that constitute international relations. It also de-emphasizes questions of who-gets-what in order to stress systemic processes and functions; and by overlooking matters of goals and their formulation, it thus omits a great deal of the essence of politics. Although Easton's is in many ways the most inclusive systemic approach for political analysis, its omissions limit its role to that of a framework for organizing and conceptualizing data. This is no small achievement, but yet it is one that falls well short of a general theory of politics.[18]

---

16 Burton, *Systems, States, Diplomacy and Rules,* p. 5.
17 Young, *Systems of Political Science,* pp. 19–20.
18 Ibid., pp. 46–48.

Almond's structural-functional approach has also been subject to criticism. It has been observed to share with Easton's approach a tendency (at least among its practitioners) to distort reality in the interests of conceptual neatness. It has also been criticized as excessively static in analysis and prone to rationalize status quo patterns by its efforts to demonstrate the functionality of existing arrangements. This propensity toward a "what is is good" bias is not necessarily inseparable from functional analysis, but Young observes that on balance the nature of this approach makes it easy to slip into conservative patterns and biases.[19]

In broader terms, what is the overall utility of general systems theory? Essentially it is that the construct provides a conceptual framework but not an actual theory. A. James Gregor has observed that to speak of an individual, a family, a church, an army, or a polity as a "system" is to do no more than speak metaphorically. Systems theory and functional analysis leave us with metaphors and analogies that serve essentially classificatory purposes. These analyses are not explanatory or predictive so much as they are analytic and heuristic. As Gregor comments, Easton's definition of a system as "any set of variables regardless of the degree of interrelationship among them," is so loose that it would be difficult to find occasions when a system no longer exists.[20] And whereas a theory makes empirical knowledge claims, an analytic conceptual scheme is little more than a nontheoretical classificatory tool. Indeed, Gregor notes that Easton refers to his systems analysis as a "conceptual framework" that is a "preliminary to the development of theory" and as a way of framing "appropriate questions" and possibilities for seeking answers rather than providing actual answers.[21] Thus general systems theory's main contribution is not as a theory but as a means of classification and a way of stimulating thought. On the other hand, the systems perspective may also provide a skeleton upon which a general theory of world politics might be constructed, in contrast to previous theories, which have mainly been confined to the level of intergovernmental relationships.[22] To

---

[19] Ibid., pp. 35–37.

[20] A. James Gregor, "Political Science and the Uses of Functional Analysis," *American Political Science Review* 62 (June 1968): 431. Easton's definition is from *A System Analysis of Political Life*, op. cit., p. 21.

[21] Gregor, "Political Science," p. 435.

[22] Banks, "Systems Analysis," p. 350.

explore this and other possibilities in the application of systems theory, this chapter must now turn to the level of the international political system.

II. Is There an International Political System?

Is there an international political system? If so, what are its characteristics and to what uses may the conception of it be put? The initial question requires careful consideration, since to employ the concept in the absence of a legitimate theoretical or empirical justification would be to vitiate the systems theory enterprise as far as the study of international relations is concerned. For example, it has been asked if there truly is "a polity answering to the name of Nigeria, Rhodesia, Kenya, Tanzania, the Dominican Republic, . . . ?" [23] If we employ a minimal definition of a system as a set of units in interaction, it is possible to conceive of relations among nations as constituting a kind of system. And David Easton has observed that at the international level there are to be found sets of relations through which values are authoritatively allocated, though he recognizes that unlike other systems, the international system lacks strong legitimacy feelings. Easton argues that members do make demands with the expectation that these will be met, that international life has a culture that is more than the sum of its component national cultures, and that although authorities in the international political system are less centralized and more fragile, the more powerful countries as well as bodies such as the United Nations have met with at least partial success in resolving national differences and in having the various allocations accepted as authoritative (even if not always legitimate). Indeed, Easton concludes that there exists an international political system no more unique or atypical than any other system. [24] Apart from Easton's observations, it is also possible to note that while the international system lacks any real degree of authority, there are at least rudimentary elements of emergent international consensus. Among these elements are widespread agreement that survival is preferable to nuclear devastation, that at least partially autonomous

---

[23] Mackenzie, *Politics and Social Science*, p. 109.
[24] Easton, *A Systems Analysis of Political Life*, pp. 485–87.

units organized along territorial lines are the basic components of the system, that most mutual contacts (e.g., trade, tourism, diplomatic exchange) are conducted on a regulated and commonly accepted basis, that some degree of general interdependence exists (as reflected in the UN, World Court, World Health Organization, and various functional, regional and intergovernmental organizations), and even that certain elements of universal morality may be dimly perceived.[25] Nor is this interdependence entirely remote and theoretical. W.J.M. Mackenzie aptly observes that "A child hurt in the streets of Saigon may be related, by a fairly short series of steps, to risks involving children in Haiti or Greenland, as well as in New York, Moscow and Peking."[26]

While it may be true that a system, like beauty, is in the eye of the beholder,[27] there is, nonetheless, a more reliable way to consider whether international relations or world politics—conceived of as the pattern of relations between individual nations—constitutes anything more than a minimal system; it is to test the concept of the international political system against the four functions that, according to Parsonian theory, any social system must fulfill. The first of these, pattern maintenance, is definitely carried out, since the pattern of interaction among nations has been maintained and would only be altered by the unlikely establishment of world government or a new world empire equivalent to that of the Romans. Nuclear holocaust is, however, a potential threat to this function. The pattern-maintenance function is also evidenced by the performance of the system and its members in tending to uphold the independence of the various component parts. Adaptation is the second function, and while the international political system may not be coping exceptionally well with its changing environment— both physical and political—the function is, nonetheless, being carried out. The third function, goal attainment, is also being performed in rudimentary form, in the sense of system survival, though periodic efforts at international aid and cooperation, as well as efforts to channel or to limit violence, occasionally provide evidence

---

[25] See Ivo Duchacek, *Nations and Men*, 2d ed. (New York: Holt, 1971), pp. 100–1.

[26] Mackenzie, *Politics and Social Science*, p. 360.

[27] J. David Singer, "The Global System and Its Subsystems: A Developmental View," in James N. Rosenau, ed., *Linkage Politics: Essays on The Convergence of National and International Systems* (New York: The Free Press, 1969), p. 22n.

that this function is more than minimal. Finally, there is integration. Here the parts of the system have sometimes operated in opposition to each other (even to the point of threatening each other's survival), while simultaneously they may engage in cooperation through international bodies. Thus the relations between the United States and the Soviet Union display both kinds of behavior. In essence, the integrative function is also carried out in at least a weak manner.

The conclusion therefore must be that while international relations, in terms of an international political system, are not characterized by a high degree of coherence or centralized authority, nor always by clear boundaries, they nonetheless meet more than the minimum definitional requirements for designation as a system. There is, in other words, an international political system.

During the past decade there has been considerable serious effort to treat international relations as an international political system and to delineate its characteristics. McClelland, for example, notes that the individual nation is a complex of related physical and human activities. To sustain itself it must direct most of its energies inward, but it also requires some exchange with its environment. This exchange between nations constitutes international relations. From a system perspective, all the activity on the part of nations in taking from and giving to the international environment is considered together and may be called the international system.[28] At any time in history this international system is in a particular condition, or state, marked by a specific form, structure, and processes, all of which are the subject of study. With the passage of time the international system evolves from one such state to another, and these transformations are also an important object of inquiry, as are characteristics such as input, output, environmental exchange, homeostasis, and system performance. Among these components, inputs consist of those factors that influence the international system and may lead to changes within it, and outputs are the response to these stimuli. The systems perspective also permits attention to non-state actors such as religious bodies, alliances, international

---

[28] McClelland, *Theory and the International System*, p. 90. For a textbook definition, that of William D. Coplin seems useful: "The international political system is a system of states, each of which claims control within its boundaries and acts to maintain that control domestically and internationally." *Introduction to International Politics: A Theoretical Overview* (Chicago: Markham, 1971), p. 296.

organizations, and other groups that exist within or across national lines and that may have some effect upon the international system. The criteria for determining the components of the international system are merely that such units be able to decide and act internationally, that they interact with other actors and have an impact on their calculations, and that they persist over time.[29]

Another analytic concept utilized within the systems approach is that of the international subsystem. This can be defined as "a pattern of relations among basic units in world politics which exhibits a particular degree of regularity and intensity of relations as well as awareness of interdependence among the participating units." [30] Thus such areas as the Middle East, Western Europe, or Central America can be treated as international subsystems. The value of the subsystem orientation may be considerable because it encourages theory and research on these levels and facilitates a comparative dimension as well as retention of a broader perspective.[31]

III. The International Political System: Some Theoretical Applications

To what use may the concept of the international political system be applied? Basically, it provides a significant series of related questions and perspectives for scholarly inquiry. First, in contrast to many traditional approaches that have focused upon national actions, largely in terms of foreign policy making, it directs attention to national interactions at the level of the international system or subsystem. Second, by providing a comprehensive framework with a hierarchy of systems and subsystems, it provides opportunities to relate (or to undertake research upon) events and processes

---

[29] See Andrew M. Scott, *The Functioning of the International Political System* (New York: Macmillan, 1967), p. 27.

[30] Karl Kaiser, "The Interaction of Regional Subsystems: Some Preliminary Notes on Recurrent Patterns and the Role of Superpowers," *World Politics*, 21 (October 1968): 86.

[31] See, for example, Louis J. Cantori and Steven L. Spiegel, eds., *The International Politics of Regions: A Comparative Approach* (Englewood Cliffs, N.J.: Prentice-Hall, 1970), and *International Studies Quarterly* (December 1969), special issue on International Subsystems.

that take place at different levels. Third, it offers a perspective from which to conceive of certain kinds of national behavior as a function of the international system, rather than vice-versa. The considerations of system-generated conflict and conflict reduction in game theory (particularly Chicken and Prisoner's Dilemma), in cybernetics, and in some portions of conflict theory exemplify this. Fourth, the systems approach may afford a more fruitful perspective from which to perceive phenomena such as alliances, crises, and wars in terms of their effects as disturbances upon the international system. In these cases it directs attention to the question of whether system equilibrium is restored and in what manner the disturbances are met (i.e., homeostatic response). Fifth, the systems approach may have the potential for revealing how systems transformations actually come about. It also encourages attention to systematic consideration of the characteristics of different international systems over time, and to the identification of historical and behavioral patterns. Whether or not these may be called laws of operation is another matter, but Coplin notes that recurrent activity patterns may be identified, as in the case of threats to the system being met by states acting collectively, and in the example of constant penetration of states into each other's affairs.[32]

Partisans of the systemic approach hold that useful knowledge will develop from these kinds of efforts and that this knowledge will lead to improved description, explanation, prediction, and even control of international politics.[33] This, then, is the promise, but what in practice have the actual applications of systems theory to international relations produced?

Systems theory has, in a variety of ways, guided the theorizing (and sometimes the research) of a large number of scholars: Morton Kaplan, Richard Rosecrance, John Burton, Charles McClelland, J. David Singer, Karl Deutsch, K. J. Holsti, George Modelski, and others. However, Kaplan's models deserve primary attention here since he has constructed one of the earliest, most extensive, and most well-known frameworks.

Kaplan has created a number of "macromodels" of international

---

[32] Coplin, *Introduction to International Politics*, p. 296.

[33] For example, McClelland finds that systems theory may make it possible to understand the outcome when two or more contrary efforts to control the international system are exerted at the same time. *Theory and the International System*, p. 91.

politics, based on several underlying assumptions: first, that a
pattern of repeatable or characteristic behavior occurs within the
international system; second, that this behavior exhibits a pattern
because its elements are consistent and because they fulfill national
and international needs; third, that patterns of institutional behavior are related in specific ways to the type of actors taking part
in international politics; and fourth, that international behavior can
also be related to military, economic, technological, demographic,
and other factors.[34] Just as sociologists have found it possible to
build alternative models of family systems (nuclear, extended,
polygamous), and political scientists have dealt with different
models of political systems (democratic, totalitarian), so according
to Kaplan it is possible to construct various models of the international system. Accordingly, he differentiates six different models
largely on the basis of degree of integration and number of actors.
Kaplan is careful to note that these are macromodels of international politics, not models of the foreign policy process, nor of
regional or national systems, so that one should not criticize them
on the basis of exaggerated expectations involving other levels. Thus
a model meant to apply to the international political system as a
whole could not be expected to explain developments within a given
regional subsystem such as Africa, any more than an economic
model treating monopolism could be expected "to explain the
economics of the garment trade on the East Coast of the United
States."[35] Similarly, Kaplan cautions that the models are merely
tools for investigating reality. And as for predictions of specific
events, he observes that a theory of international politics probably
cannot produce a forecast of an occurrence such as the 1956
Hungarian Revolution, but that we ought not to make such a
demand of theory. Because international interactions are too
complex and the number of free variables too great, international
political theory is unable to predict individual actions, but Kaplan
does find it possible to expect it to predict characteristic behavior

---

[34] Morton A. Kaplan, "Balance of Power, Bipolarity and Other Models of
International Systems," *American Political Science Review* 51 (September
1957): 684. The basic statement of Kaplan's approach can be found here
and in *System and Process,* op. cit.; it is also restated in Kaplan, ed., *New
Approaches to International Relations* (New York: St. Martin's Press, 1968),
especially pp. 381–404; and in his *Macropolitics* (Chicago: Aldine, 1969),
especially pp. 209–42.
[35] Kaplan, *New Approaches to International Politics,* p. 385.

in particular kinds of international systems, and also the conditions under which a system will remain stable or be transformed.[36]

Kaplan's actual models reflect the assumption that the structure of a complex system tends to determine its characteristic performance. He does not claim that his six models exhaust the possible international configurations. Instead they are points on a scale of organization from the smallest to the highest degree of political integration. Two of the models, labeled "balance of power" and "loose bipolar" are historical, but the other four are merely projections based on the requirements of internal consistency and relationship to other political and economic factors. They embody possible transformations of the presently existing loose bipolar model, and they also represent "possible predictions of the theory when the transformations are explicitly linked to the conditions that will bring them into being." [37] These four nonhistorical models are the "tight bipolar" system (i.e., bipolarity in which each of two major powers leads a bloc of allied states that it completely dominates, and in a situation where international organizations are very weak and there are no neutrals); the "universal" system (which is a federal world state based on principles of mutual toleration and universal rule of law); the "hierarchical" system (involving a single world state created by a nation's conquest or by a democratic arrangement replacing territorial units with functional ones); and finally a "unit veto" system (or multipolarity characterized by each state possessing sufficient nuclear forces to deter any other state from attacking it).[38] For all six of his models of the international system, Kaplan formulates hypotheses, particularly concerning the conditions of each model's maintenance or self-preservation, as well as the conditions surrounding the behavior of states within it and the possible transformation to other system forms. Each model is designated in terms of "essential rules" describing the characteristic behavior necessary to preserve system equilibrium. There are also four other sets of variables for each model: these are the "transformation rules," which set out the system changes that occur as inputs move the system toward instability or a new system; "actor clas-

---

[36] Kaplan, "Balance of Power, Bipolarity and Other Models," pp. 684–85.
[37] Ibid., pp. 685–86.
[38] The parenthetical descriptions are based on the welcome contribution of Ernst Haas, who has "retranslated" Kaplan's systems "into everyday terms." *Beyond the Nation-State*, pp. 57–58.

sificatory variables," which state the actors' structural characteristics; "capability variables"; and "information variables." [39]

Of the two historical systems, the loose bipolar one is implicitly a
model of the international system in the generation after World
War II, in which each of the two superpowers headed an alliance
of varying cohesion, while numbers of neutral states and international organizations also existed. The "essential rules" here include
the following:

1. Blocs strive to increase their relative capabilities.
2. Blocs tend to be willing to run at least some risks to eliminate rival
   blocs.
3. Blocs tend to engage in major war rather than to permit rival blocs
   to attain predominance.
4. Blocs tend to subordinate objectives of the universal actor to objectives of the bloc but subordinate objectives of rival blocs to the
   universal actor.
5. Nonbloc actors tend to support the universal actor generally and
   specifically against contrary objectives of blocs.
6. Nonbloc actors tend to act to reduce the danger of war between
   blocs.
7. Nonbloc actors tend to be neutral between blocs except where important objectives of the universal actor are involved.
8. Blocs attempt to extend membership but tend to tolerate the status
   of nonbloc actors.[40]

The balance of power model is the one that has received the most
attention, and it describes a system of at least five powers in which
there is no authoritative international organization. The implicit
reference point here is eighteenth and nineteenth century Europe.
There are six "essential rules" for this system:

1. Act to increase capabilities but negotiate rather than fight.
2. Fight rather than pass up an opportunity to increase capabilities.
3. Stop fighting rather than eliminate an essential national actor.
4. Act to oppose any coalition or single actor that tends to assume a
   position of predominance with respect to the rest of the system.
5. Act to constrain actors who subscribe to supranational organizing
   principles.
6. Permit defeated or constrained essential national actors to reenter the

---

[39] Kaplan, *Macropolitics*, pp. 212–13.
[40] Kaplan, *New Approaches to International Relations*, p. 393.

system as acceptable role partners or act to bring some previously inessential actor within the essential actor classification. Treat all essential actors as acceptable role partners.[41]

According to Kaplan, these models are meant to be merely hypothetical. He indicates that only when the balance of power system was played out on a computer, through numerous simulations, were he and his collaborators able to test its susceptibility to various parameters and to explore the interrelationship of propositions about its structure. For example the computer revealed that a balance of power system became unstable when an actor was hegemony-oriented rather than security-oriented. At first a balance-oriented actor was the victim but ultimately the hegemony-inclined actor would fail and be eliminated by others.[42] In addition, he discovered that wars tended to be four-against-one rather than three-against-two. Since this finding was contradicted by the historical record, it caused Kaplan to modify the balance of power model itself in order to increase the correspondence with reality.

Of what real value are Kaplan's systems models? In his original formulation, Kaplan himself said that, "in a strict sense," they do not constitute a theory:

A theory includes a set of primitive terms, definitions and axioms. From this base, systematic theorems are derived. These theorems should be logically consistent. The terminal theorems or propositions should be interpreted in such a way that the terms of the theorems can be given unequivocal empirical references. Finally, the theorems should be capable of refutation or confirmation by means of controlled experiment or systematic observation. If "theory" is interpreted in this sense, this book does not contain a theory.[43]

Yet the disclaimer was less than total, for he went on to assert that if the criteria for a theory were relaxed, then this was a kind of theory after all:

If some of the requirements for a theory are loosened; if systematic completeness is not required; if proof of logical consistency is not required; if unambiguous interpretation of terms and laboratory methods

---

[41] Ibid., p. 391.
[42] Ibid., pp. 385–86.
[43] Kaplan, *System and Process*, p. xi.

of confirmation are not required; then this book is, or at least contains, a theory. *This theory may be viewed as an initial or introductory theory of international politics.*[44]

In the ensuing decade, Kaplan's models came under substantial criticism, and while he persisted in upholding the validity of his original six hypothetical models subject to some lesser variations, he appears to have modified his attitude toward their theoretical significance. The systems models are now to be regarded as only "tools for investigating reality"; Kaplan tells us that the models he first developed were "quite crude," and that they rested on no more than "plausible reasoning."[45] Since the models are hypothetical, their main function appears to be heuristic, in the sense of calling attention to other possible system types and to particular kinds of inquiry that theorists and researchers ought to make.

Another limitation of Kaplan's approach, as he himself observes, is that the models face the difficulty of a trade-off between generality and reality. Thus if important economic, political, technological and personality factors were incorporated, the models would become so complex that efforts to discuss and relate them systematically would bog down in detail.[46] But in their present form, are the models any more than what a severe critic of Kaplan's work has called merely "an intellectual exercise and no more"?[47] To arrive at a reliable evaluation is not easy, and the task is in no way facilitated by Kaplan's style, which has been labeled discursive, imprecise and pretentious.[48] Granted that the models are said to be only "hypothetical," they still display a number of shortcomings. For one thing, they are structured so that behavior within them is determined by the system itself, in terms of the number of national actors and the power configurations among them. National and subnational causes of action are virtually ignored.[49] To be sure,

---

[44] Ibid., italics added.

[45] Kaplan, *Macropolitics,* p. 210.

[46] Kaplan, *New Approaches,* p. 389.

[47] Hedley Bull, "International Theory: The Case for a Classical Approach," *World Politics* 17 (April 1966): 372.

[48] See William Welch's review of *Macropolitics,* in *The American Political Science Review* 65 (June 1971): 511–12.

[49] See, e.g., the criticisms of Ernst Haas, *Beyond the Nation-State,* p. 58; and Stanley Hoffman, "The Long Road to Theory," *World Politics* 11 (April 1959): 346–77.

significant amounts of national actions and international interactions are caused by the nature of an international system (alliance behavior within a balance of power system would be an example of this); nonetheless the exclusion of subsystemic factors removes from consideration additional critical factors such as regional relationships; internal crises; decision-making processes; the nature of group, class, or political pressures; entire socio-economic patterns; and ideology. The omission of these last two variables presents particular problems. For the models to be of more than limited value, socio-economic factors must be incorporated unless it can be demonstrated that the level of organization (whether tribal, agrarian, industrializing, or fully industrialized) is irrelevant to broad patterns of national and international behavior. Together with the omission of distinctly political and ideological factors this means that the models, as Ernst Haas has observed, are "far too rigidly theological in their mania for stability, equilibrium and self-maintenance to serve as dynamic stimuli for projection." [50]

From a more narrowly methodological standpoint, the Kaplan systems models have further weaknesses. There is no priority among the variables, so that it is difficult to judge which are most important. The models are also formulated at too general a level to be of much use in the ordering of facts.[51] Finally, while claiming to predict behavior within a particular kind of international system, they do not extend much beyond the level of definition, in that the distinction between proposition and definition is not clearly drawn.

The usefulness of Kaplan's systems theory thus exists only within rather limited heuristic lines, but what of other approaches to the international political system? Some of these have already been considered in earlier chapters, since the approaches to conflict of Rummel, of Wilkenfeld, and of Deutsch and Singer, as well as the work with transactions indices,[52] all represent applications of a systems approach. Hence a number of additional efforts will only be alluded to briefly here. Among these is the use by K. J. Holsti of a systems approach to classify and provide an orderly framework for treatment of historical material. Holsti treats as an international system any collection of independent political entities—from tribes

---

[50] Haas, *Beyond the Nation-State*, p. 65.
[51] See McClelland, *Theory and the International System*, p. 24.
[52] See chapters four and five of this work.

to empires—that interact with frequency on the basis of regularized processes. He analyzes historical systems according to five aspects: boundaries separating the area of interaction from its environment, the main characteristics of the political units involved, the structure or configuration of power and influence, forms of interaction, and rules or customs. This allows him to proceed with an orderly discussion and comparison of systems as diverse as the Chou dynasty in China, the Greek city-state system, and the various European state systems of the last several centuries.[53] Another approach is to concentrate upon regional subsystems. Cantori and Spiegel find several advantages inherent in this regional focus. First, instead of dealing with the 150 or more states making up the international political system, they need deal only with fifteen regional units. Second, this procedure broadens the horizons of area specialists and also permits an improved comprehension of individual areas for the generalist. Third, it may provide a broader grasp of the interaction of various parts and levels of the international system. And fourth, it facilitates comparative study of both contemporary and historical systems.[54]

The approaches of Holsti and of Cantori and Spiegel are primarily classificatory, but other efforts have sought to apply systems theory more ambitiously. Thus Richard Rosecrance has divided the period from 1740 to 1960 into nine distinct international systems and then separated these into two categories as stable and unstable systems.[55] His main finding is that the explanation for transformations in the international system involves a correlation between international instability and actor disturbances (particularly the domestic insecurity of elites). However the Rosecrance study, in common with others such as that of Kaplan, makes sharp (and possibly unwarranted) distinctions between international systems in different periods. A recent systematic analysis of membership in intergovernmental organizations over time has found the global system to be a single evolving entity rather than a sequence of distinct systems divided by sharp temporal boundaries. And major

---

[53] Holsti, *International Politics: A Framework for Analysis* (Englewood Cliffs, N.J.: Prentice-Hall, 1967), pp. 27 ff.
[54] Cantori and Spiegel, *International Politics of Regions*, pp. 3–5.
[55] Richard N. Rosecrance, *Action and Reaction in World Politics* (Boston: Little, Brown, 1963).

transformations that do occur are not abrupt but gradual.[56] There is also a conceptual disadvantage in postulating different international systems over time. The difficulty is that dividing lines are necessarily uncertain and the source of continual reexamination, and that interests in different systemic properties may be the source of different sets of differentiations.[57]

IV. The Possibilities and Limitations of Systems Theory

The systems approach to the study of international politics combines a body of theoretical assumptions about systemic relationships with a method of analysis that seeks to apply it to the subject at hand. The conception of the international political system that this approach fosters may be said to provide certain real benefits. Obviously the approach has heuristic value in that it prompts the asking of new questions and the adoption of different perspectives toward an old subject. While many different kinds of theoretical approaches have heuristic value regardless of their shortcomings, the systems orientation certainly has caused a major widening in the scope of scholarly inquiry. But beyond this, it has also encouraged a certain emphasis on formalization as part of a self-conscious adoption of a more social-scientific approach. This orientation has brought about the introduction of a specialized vocabulary and classificatory scheme for the ordering of information. It has also facilitated the carrying out of scholarly inquiry at different systemic levels without losing sense of the interrelationship among these levels. In addition, the systems orientation has the potential for generating hypotheses and for sharing in a process of mutual stimulus, modification and reinforcement between theory and empirical work. For example, it can be argued that the systems framework has stimulated recent studies of political integration and is being reinforced by them as the studies produce empirical evidence of complex interrelationships between systemic

---

[56] Michael D. Wallace, "Clusters of Nations in the Global System, 1865–1964: Some Preliminary Evidence," paper presented at the Annual Meeting of the International Studies Association (Western Region), San Francisco, March 26–27, 1971, p. 15.

[57] See the comments of J. David Singer, "The Global System and Its Subsystems," pp. 30–31.

levels, which general systems theory had suggested.[58] Finally, through its concern with questions of pattern maintenance it directs attention to broad patterns of stability and change, and by emphasizing a world-wide perspective, it encourages movement away from narrowly conceived foreign policy studies and toward a significant international interdependence.

A number of the limitations of the systems approaches have already been assessed in the discussion of general systems theory and in the evaluation of Kaplan's approach, but important points remain to be made about their present state and significance. The first limitation is that, as Easton and Kaplan have acknowledged, the systems approaches are not yet theories but only conceptual frameworks. Perhaps, then, it is not surprising that none of the systems frameworks has been able to lay down intellectual policy for the international relations theory field nor precipitate the empirical research necessary to validate it.[59]

The second major limitation of the systems approach involves methodological inadequacy. The lack of operationalization of concepts in a way that would make them accessible to empirical testing is a particular difficulty. As Brams acidly observes:

Not even useful by-products, not to mention theories, can emerge
. . . from models that cannot fail (i.e. are irrefutable because their
concepts are not operationally defined and propositions linking the
concepts therefore cannot be tested empirically). A necessary condition
for the advancement of a science is that it provide for self-corrective
mechanisms that permit confirmation or disconfirmation of empirical
propositions suggested by a model. A model . . . from which testable
propositions cannot be derived that would refute it can stand only as
a monument to an abstraction untrammeled by reality.[60]

System relationships are often unspecified, and the entanglement between definitions and propositions presents further problems.

---

58 Banks, "Systems Analysis," p. 350.
59 Charles McClelland, cited in K. J. Holsti, "Retreat from Utopia: International Relations Theory, 1945–1970," paper presented at the Sixty-sixth Annual Meeting of the American Political Science Association, Los Angeles, California, September 8–12, 1970, p. 10.
60 Steven J. Brams, "The Search for Structural Order in the International System: Some Preliminary Models and Results," *International Studies Quarterly* 13 (September 1969): 279.

For example, the main function in one particular systems model is essentially identical to its chief attribute, which is the safeguarding of the independence of the international system and the maintenance of order by minimizing force and violence.[61] In addition, Charles McClelland has observed that much of the earlier work in this field overlooked some fundamental problems of definition, particularly concerning social, economic and political attributes of the components (i.e., nations) of the international system, and also in defining properties, or interaction characteristics, of the system. Thus there remains a major "linkage problem" of explaining relationships between component attributes and relational properties in the system, with a view to determining whether their relationship is sensitive to some pattern, is determined by an important intervening variable, involves some attribute not yet selected, or perhaps does not exist at all. Resolving this kind of relationship could help to answer a question such as whether the incidence and severity of warfare is in some way related to certain kinds of national characteristics. Also within the category of methodology is the matter of language. The borrowing of concepts and terminology from other social sciences has created problems of its own, and resulted in what has been called a "sometimes barbarous academic vocabulary which is used to redescribe reasonably well-confirmed or intuitively grasped low order empirical generalizations." [62] While this complaint of jargon is not peculiar to the area of systems theory, and a specialized vocabulary is a necessary part of social-scientific formalization, the thrust of the criticism is more than esthetic, for the use of jargon does on occasion function as a substitute for analysis and explanation.

The third major limitation of the systems approach revolves around the gap between theory and research. Systems-oriented theorizing has not until very recently led to a great deal of empirical work. This unfortunate bifurcation between theory and research has sharply limited the usefulness and value of systems theory. As J. David Singer has commented:

Theory may be the intelligent man's substitution for empiricism, but when so much of our theory is little better than superstition (tribal, at

---

[61] The point is made by Ernst Haas, *Beyond the Nation-State*, p. 63, with reference to a model of George Modelski, but it is also applicable to some other models.

[62] A. James Gregor, "Political Science," p. 438.

that) and so much depends on accurate knowledge, we cannot afford to ignore the inductive road to such knowledge.[63]

There are, however, indications of a recent trend in the discipline away from more grandiose theorizing and toward empirical research that is directed by theoretical considerations.[64]

Still another limitation of the systems approaches concerns what they omit of the stuff of politics. That is, they are not conducive to the consideration or the study of political institutions, political culture, and other critical domestic variables, nor do they give scope to historical and ideological factors. And the gross categorization that generality requires may be purchased at too great a cost, so that to conceive of Malawi or Luxembourg as international actors in the sense that the United States, Britain, or China are so regarded seriously distorts one's analytic perspective.

It would be convenient to conclude an appraisal of the systems approach with a kind of balanced verdict that does no more than contrast potentialities and accomplishments with past and present limitations. But the difficulties of utilization, whether inherent or due to problems of application and conceptualization at the present stage of the discipline, make it hard to avoid agreeing with the evaluation of George Modelski. He concludes that for some practitioners of systems theory the very utterance of the "magic term 'system' has become a ritual act of special potency, expected to confer upon the utterer instant admission not only to the circle of the initiated but also to a 'sesame' of political wisdom." [65] The initial systems approaches have lent themselves to much avoidable mystification, and this in a field already suffering from the earlier "mind-beclouding" concepts of power, sovereignty and statehood:

In brief, although systems analysis, has, in part, prepared the ground for a geocentric approach, the question may legitimately be put whether its usefulness is not now at an end. The study of the politics of world

---

[63] Singer, "The Global System and Its Subsystems," p. 30. Oran Young also calls attention to this dichotomy between "hyperfactualism" and "excessive theorizing." *Systems of Political Science*, p. 94.

[64] See Charles A. McClelland, "Driving Out the Hollowness: The Reshaping of International Systems Theory," mimeographed, University of Southern California, March 1968.

[65] Modelski, "The Promise of Geocentric Politics," p. 631.

societies is moving into a phase in which the simple "system" label no longer carries meaningful connotations.[66]

The analysis of international politics has undoubtedly gained from the contributions of systems theory, but given on the one hand the above limitations and on the other the presence of alternative techniques and approaches suitable for theory and research, the present tendency toward empirical work (informed by theory) and away from gross systems speculation appears to be a healthy development.

BIBLIOGRAPHY

BURTON, JOHN W. *Systems, States, Diplomacy and Rules.* Cambridge, England: Cambridge University Press, 1968. A systems approach to international relations, which views world society as clusters of state systems, some of which cut across national boundaries.

CANTORI, LOUIS J., and SPIEGEL, STEVEN L., eds. *The International Politics of Regions: A Comparative Approach.* Englewood Cliffs, N.J.: Prentice-Hall, 1970. A subsystem approach as the basis for viewing international politics.

EASTON, DAVID. *The Political System: An Inquiry Into the State of Political Science,* 2d ed. New York: Knopf, 1971. The fundamental statement of the case for systems theory in Political Science. Does not treat international politics *per se.*

————. *A Systems Analysis of Political Life.* New York: Wiley, 1965. Easton's theoretical elaboration of systems concepts to make them more applicable to empirical situations.

KAPLAN, MORTON A. *System and Process in International Politics.* New York: Wiley, 1957. One of the first large-scale works on world politics from the perspective of systems theory.

MCCLELLAND, CHARLES A. *Theory and the International System.* New York: Macmillan, 1966. A readable presentation of the systems approach at the introductory level.

ROSECRANCE, RICHARD. *Action and Reaction in World Politics.* Boston:

---

[66] Ibid., p. 633.

Little, Brown, 1963. Delineates nine models of the international system between 1740 and 1960.

ROSENAU, JAMES N., ed. *Linkage Politics: Essays on the Convergence of National and International Systems.* New York: The Free Press, 1969. Twelve original essays, which treat aspects of the linkage between national and international politics.

YOUNG, ORAN R. *Systems of Political Science.* Englewood Cliffs, N.J.: Prentice-Hall, 1968. Thoughtful treatment of problems and possibilities inherent in various systems approaches to political analysis. Occupies a "middle ground" between full theories and simple perspectives.

7

Conclusion

The preceding chapters have explored the areas of game theory, integration theory, communication theory, approaches to power and conflict, and systems theory. Together these fields exhibit many of the representative characteristics of contemporary systematic theorizing in international relations. The purpose of this concluding chapter is to provide a brief treatment of some general strengths and weaknesses of the scientific or behavioral approaches, then to raise the fundamental question of the relationship between theories of international relations and realities of world politics, and finally to offer some conclusions about the possibilities and promises of the theoretical enterprise.

I. Tradition Versus Science in International Relations Theory

Debate over the feasibility of a social-scientific approach toward the subject matter of international relations, as earlier toward political science itself, has lessened markedly as it has become clear that there could be little doubt in the possibility of such an undertaking. The significant dialogue over the nature and purpose of the study of international relations now concerns the refinement and realization of the scientific approach, and the possibilities of linking the analytic techniques and scientific rigor of the contemporary approaches with the historical, philosophical, and normative orientations of the older school.

Criticisms of the scientific shortcomings of the behavioral approach have come from those strongly committed to a scientific orientation as well as from others utterly opposed to it. Their observations overlap to a certain extent and the criticisms can be grouped into several major categories. Voices are raised against what is sometimes an excessive preoccupation with methodology,

146

and those receiving their initial exposure to the field occasionally balk at what appears to be an obsessive concern with how to go about theory and research on international relations, rather than with actual substantive work. This criticism does have a basis for justification, and there has been a marked tendency to concentrate upon scientific methodology as virtually an end in itself rather than a means to an end. Yet the transition to a scientific orientation compels some degree of methodological self-consciousness, and there has recently been an impressive growth in empirical studies characterized by both methodological sophistication and theoretical significance.

A companion problem to that of methodological excesses is reflected in the charge of jargon or obscurity in writing. Where once the traditional literature could be read and comprehended by a nonspecialized audience, now an increasingly technical and arcane vocabulary, as well as the increased use of statistical techniques, have made much of the contemporary literature inaccessible to educated laymen and sometimes even to scholars not specialized in the discipline. Of course the more traditional literature has not been unmarked by bad writing, conceptual fuzziness, and even obfuscation, but, basically, disciplinary refinement and rigor have been purchased at the price of making the audience narrower and more specialized. This has been the experience of the natural sciences, and it has become increasingly common in the social sciences. To be sure, there is still good writing and bad writing; a number of important contemporary theorists marshal their arguments with style, grace and wit, while others have willfully or by inadvertance sinned against the English language. Since some jargon is unavoidable, and given the fact that obtuseness of presentation is not limited to any one camp, a more germane indictment is that much of the specialized language has been inconsistent or imprecise. The real problem, as Michael Haas incisively observes, is the lack of authoritative definition and clarification of concepts, and as a result the same terminology means different things to different behavioralists. This failure to establish effective and standardized communication directly impedes the growth of science.[1]

From the standpoint of more rigorous scientific standards, there

---

[1] Michael Haas, "A Plea for Bridge-Building in International Relations," in Klaus Knorr and James N. Rosenau, eds., *Contending Approaches to International Politics* (Princeton, N.J.: Princeton University Press, 1969), pp. 169–70.

is another shortcoming in that the behavioral work often displays marked scientific inadequacies. Marion J. Levy, a zealous proponent of scientific rigor rebukes not only Hedley Bull, who is hostile to the scientific approach, but also Morton Kaplan, who staunchly propounds it. Kaplan's view of science is said to be "ignorant" and we are told that he "appears to feel that it is all right to be unscientific if one is sufficiently *proscientific*." [2] Levy also lists over a dozen common scientific fallacies that he claims are to be found in the work of even the most highly praised theorists and researchers.[3] Another, perhaps more balanced, critic has described common weaknesses in the use of statistical techniques,[4] and a comprehensive survey of existing behavioral research on the United Nations has described these studies as disappointing in terms of their fuzzy-mindedness, exaltation of technique over substance, dearth of cumulativeness, and lack of theory-building.[5] More could be made of these weaknesses, but scientific sophistication does appear to be on the increase and the concern for improved performance in this regard is a basic reason for the continued emphasis on methodology.

Finally, there is a question of the relationship of the behavioral studies to more traditional concerns. It has been argued that the

---

[2] Marion J. Levy, Jr., " 'Does It Matter If He's Naked?' Bawled the Child," in Knorr and Rosenau, *Contending Approaches*, p. 88.

[3] Levy discusses the following fallacies: misplaced dichotomies, teleology, misplaced engineering, allegedly extra-conscious motivation, misconceived serendipity, inutile measurement, sentimental experimentalism, reification, pathetic fallacy, circular concepts, definition by authority, indeterminate representation, and abandoned models. Ibid., pp. 94 ff. Also see Levy's "Methodology: A Means or a Field?" in Edwin H. Fedder, ed., *Methodological Concerns in International Studies* (St. Louis: University of Missouri, Center for International Studies, August 1970), pp. 137–46.

[4] Edward R. Tufte, "Improving Data Analysis in Political Science," *World Politics* 21 (July 1969): 640–54. Tufte criticizes the faddish use and misuse of certain techniques, particularly correlation coefficients (which are often inappropriate compared with multiple regression and scattergrams), and significance tests (which merely sanctify, rather than indicate what is important). He also calls attention to the problem of multicollinearity, in which two independent variables correlate very closely and it is difficult to determine which is causative (e.g., the question of whether economic development or social mobilization is more closely associated with military intervention in Latin America).

[5] Robert E. Riggs, et al., "Behavioralism in the Study of the United Nations," *World Politics* 22 (January 1970): 230.

social-scientific approach loses sight of what is *political*, that it distorts political realities, fails to take account of human purpose and aspiration, concentrates on trivia, and is unreceptive to more traditional insights and writings. There is no mistaking the fact that many of these shortcomings are serious and do characterize portions of the contemporary work. Yet some of the best behavioral work has in fact been informed by traditional problems or insights, and the resulting linkage between the two orientations produces work that is of real merit, manifestly superior to both traditional studies that have raised significant questions but lacked scientific rigor and also to behavioral research that has shown imagination and strength in technique but a lack of perspective in treating meaningful subject matter. The value of this work,[6] together with the waning of contention over the possibility of a scientific approach to international relations has elicited an important effort to join the contributions of the traditionalists to the methods and commitment to science of the behavioralists. There is thus, at least within the field of international relations, a real possibility of bridging the gap within the intellectual world between those two warring camps of "ignorant humanists" and "insensitive scientists."[7] As J. David Singer has commented, in what one may hope will prove to be the epitaph to the "Great Debate":

If we modernists can master the substantive, normative, and judgmental end of it as well as the traditionalists are mastering the concepts and methods at our end, convergence will be completed and the "war" will not have been in vain.[8]

---

[6] J. David Singer very aptly comments about a number of bivariate relationships already demonstrated or else under present investigation:

. . . if we can discover that a common enemy unifies a nation only under certain limited conditions, that the percentage of national product going to foreign trade decreases rather than increases as productivity rises, that domestic conditions correlate with a nation's foreign policy only under special conditions, that estimates of relative military power become distorted as diplomatic tension rises, or that nations are more war-prone when their status is falling rather than rising, we must conclude that the quantifying exercises were useful.

See Singer, "The Incompleat Theorist: Insight Without Evidence," in Knorr and Rosenau, *Contending Approaches*, pp. 77–78.

[7] The terms are those of Scott Greer, *The Logic of Social Inquiry* (Chicago: Aldine, 1969), p. 198.

[8] Singer, in Knorr and Rosenau, *Contending Approaches*, p. 86.

II. Theory and Reality: The Relationship to Public Policy and Political Values

Occasioned on the one hand by the partial resolution of methodological issues and on the other by increasingly urgent political problems, a reexamination of the relationship between scholarly studies and international reality has recently grown to significant proportions. The fundamental question here concerns the relevance of advanced social-scientific theory and research to the life and death realities of international politics: the problems of devastating civil wars, political change and political order, and the possibilities of nuclear catastrophe. For example, what significance does our work have for the present and future fate of Indo-China, the Middle East, East Pakistan, or the triangular relationship of the United States, Russia, and China? These questions of applicability to the real world also require consideration of the place of values and the relationship to public policy of the social-scientific enterprise.

It is significant that calls to examine these questions and to consider a reordering of priorities have come from a number of the most important figures in the behavioral movement—David Easton, Richard Snyder, and Karl Deutsch.

Easton, in a presidential address to the American Political Science Association and in a subsequent second edition of his trial-blazing book, *The Political System,* has called attention to a "post-behavioral revolution," which is motivated by a deep concern over contemporary problems and a dissatisfaction over much of the work in political science.[9] Its "Credo of Relevance" includes such tenets as: substance must take precedence over technique; behavioral science has tended to convey an orientation of "social conservatism tempered by modest incremental change"; behavioral research must deal with human values and real human needs in a time of crisis; social scientists, as intellectuals, bear a responsibility for protecting the humane values of civilization; and the professional organizations and the universities "cannot stand apart from the

---

[9] David Easton, *The Political System* (New York: Knopf, 1971). The first edition appeared in 1953. Easton's A.P.S.A. address can be found in the *American Political Science Review* 63 (December 1969): 1051–61); it is also included in *The Political System,* 2d ed., pp. 323–48.

struggles of the day." [10] What is significant about this post-behavioral revolution is that it does not share the traditionalists' hostility to systematic methodology and to science. Instead it seeks to relate the role of science to the needs of the time without abandoning the character of science as the pursuit of empirically based knowledge.[11]

Easton finds that time is critically short and our knowledge has diverged too far from present complex realities. This situation has led to a forceful criticism, which he acknowledges:

Concern for technical competence in quantifying phenomena and testing generalizations has, in the minds of many post-behavioralists, led to the evisceration of politics. . . . Confronted in the United States by a disastrous war in Vietnam, slowly starving children, angry blacks, frightened whites, aroused vigilantes, three major political assassinations within a five-year period, student uprisings on campus, and rumors of guerrilla warfare, the behavioral scientist calmly contemplates alternative modes of analysis involving such apparently remote concepts as systems, functions, culture, games, simulation, economic models, and coalition formation.[12]

Although the previous concentration on pure research and the creation of basic knowledge was appropriate during an earlier period, the intrusive nature of these problems requires a shifting of priorities. Easton contends that we need more systematic attention to applied action-oriented work, and social-scientific knowledge ought to be applied regardless of whether we are yet fully secure in our confidence of its validity, though fortunately the work of two decades has markedly increased our fund of rigorously derived knowledge, and therefore the dependability of our policy advice should be enhanced.[13]

Easton also heeds the social science distinction between fact and value identified by Max Weber and by positivism, yet he reminds us of what has been repeatedly revealed by Weber himself, as well

[10] Easton, *The Political System*, 2d ed., pp. 324–27. Easton notes that these points constitute a Weberian ideal type which no one individual necessarily subscribes to in their entirety. For example, the point of politicization of professional organizations and universities would surely be less widely acceptable than some of the other items.
[11] Ibid., p. 363.
[12] Ibid., p. 368.
[13] Ibid., pp. 353–54.

as by Marx, Mannheim and others—that all research necessarily rests on certain value assumptions.[14] And, even if we conclude that values and facts are logically separate, Easton points out that we cannot thereby derive a moral position to exclude value judgments. He observes that the post-behavioral orientation regards knowledge and the opportunity for rational choice as imposing special obligations:

The political scientist as a professional is the knower *par excellence*. It is therefore immoral for him not to act on his knowledge. In holding that to know is to bear a responsibility for acting, post-behavioralism joins a venerable tradition inherited from such diverse sources as Greek classical philosophy, Karl Marx, John Dewey, and modern existentialism.[15]

Thus there is a normative sense in which knowledge compels action. In choosing a theoretical approach, the factor of social relevance may be a "second order or supplementary criterion" to that of scientific adequacy.[16] Easton is justifiably careful to caution that the need for commitment does not imply abandonment or even retrenchment of the search for basic knowledge; it does, however, require an adaptation of science to changing needs and a reordering of our concerns.

While Easton's formulation applies to political science broadly, there have been other important calls for a reorientation of the international relations field itself. Richard Snyder, as president of the International Studies Association, has told its members that the discipline has gotten too far from the world it would explain. To redress the balance, Snyder has called to mind the need for asking "the naive common sense questions about the world".[17] And Karl Deutsch, following the precedent established by his predecessor as president of the American Political Science Association, has addressed himself to a reordering of priorities. Deutsch identifies the

---

[14] Ibid., pp. 338 and 358. Easton provides one index of the neglect of serious social problems by political science. In the decade from 1958 to 1968, he finds that the *American Political Science Review* (the preeminent journal in the discipline) "published only 3 articles on the urban crisis; 4 on racial conflicts; 1 on poverty; 2 on civil disobedience; and 2 on violence in the U.S." p. 338.

[15] Ibid., p. 343.

[16] Ibid., p. 370.

[17] Address to the International Studies Association/West, San Francisco, California, March 27, 1971.

recent work of American political scientists as somewhat one-sided in that while it has provided serious policy advice for government, it has done far less to produce information and policy reform proposals for nongovernmental bodies such as labor unions, civic organizations, reform groups and the general public.[18]

Deutsch identifies two major issues upon which the thoughts and actions of political science must be focused during the next generation. One of these is the ending of poverty in the highly industrialized countries, the other is the eradication of large-scale war throughout the entire world. While the effort to solve these two problems may seem hopeless and the attempt even naive in view of the continuity of these phenomena through much of recorded history, Deutsch usefully reminds us that another persistent affliction, slavery, was singled out and virtually eradicated during the half-century between the 1820s and 1870s. As Easton has done, Deutsch acknowledges the relative shortage and imperfection of our professional skills, but in calling attention to the urgent need for the application of our cognitive powers to these exceptionally necessary tasks, he also stresses the fact that no one else is so equipped to undertake the work.

We thus come to the question of the propriety of orienting ourselves toward such tangible political problems. There are some who would abjure involvement with these concerns, and who regard them as mundane, a diversion from the scientific tasks of pure research, or a threat to scientific objectivity and political neutrality. These concerns are not trivial, but they are best viewed within a hierarchy of priorities. The primordial problem is quite literally one of survival. Evocations of the nuclear peril or the dangers of widespread warfare are commonplace enough so that we tend to tune them out for a variety of obvious pragmatic and psychological reasons. Perhaps the late Reinhold Niebuhr was correct when he attributed our lack of appreciation of the unique and peculiar distinction of living on the edge of catastrophe to both a lack of imaginative capacity to interpret the real meaning of the time in which we live, and to an absence of historical perspective.[19] But whatever the reason, the problems of the real world are so intrusive

---

18 Karl W. Deutsch, "On Political Theory and Political Action," *American Political Science Review* 65 (March 1971): p. 26.
19 "History's Limitations in the Nuclear Age," *The New Leader*, February 4, 1963, pp. 18–19.

that we can scarcely avoid dealing with them. Moreover, even if it is possible to foreswear involvement with these issues, this abdication invites disaster. J. David Singer aptly notes that if we defer voicing our judgments on matters of public policy until such time as our science is fully developed, there is a "fairly high risk" that these problems will have become even less manageable than they are now, or that even before then "it is not impossible" that we may "have stumbled into Armageddon." [20]

A second fundamental consideration is that of who else is to undertake the task of studying and making recommendations on critical policy questions. Deutsch has cautioned that there is a dearth of those with professional competence in political and social science, and an oversupply of "zealous partisans of competing varieties of ignorance." [21] While it may be objected that social scientists would thereby abuse their position, Singer disagrees and reminds us of some pertinent considerations and moral imperatives:

On matters of bridge design, the hazards of smoking, auto safety, construction of the SST, or real estate zoning, the specialist in international politics is no more powerful than most of his fellow citizens, with decisions inevitably made on the basis of some mix of political pressure and expertise. As retarded as our discipline may be, we have as great a right and responsibility to take public stands in our area of special competence as the engineer, medical researcher, lobbyist, sales manager, planner, or land speculator have in theirs. In my view, knowledge is meant to energize, not paralyze.[22]

Indeed, it can be added that any change from the present situation of information collection and processing at the international level could hardly be for the worse. As Boulding argues, "it is not only inadequate, it is corrupt, it is not merely a zero, it is a minus. It is an enormous apparatus designed, in fact, to produce misinformation

---

[20] In Knorr and Rosenau, *Contending Approaches*, p. 81. Kenneth Boulding has expressed the belief that the international system is so unstable as to threaten the very existence of life on earth. "National Images and International Systems," *Journal of Conflict Resolution* 3 (June 1959), in William D. Coplin and Charles W. Kegley, Jr., *A Multi-Method Introduction to International Politics* (Chicago: Markham, 1971), p. 379.

[21] Deutsch, "On Political Theory and Political Action," p. 27.

[22] In Knorr and Rosenau, *Contending Approaches*, p. 81.

and to prevent feedback from inadequate images of the world." [23] He holds that our main hope for change lies in the growth of sophistication. Intellectual investment in developing more adequate international images and theories of the international system, which would displace naive, self-centered and unsophisticated world images (held by ordinary citizens and powerful statesmen alike— both viewing nations as good or evil and wars as acts of other nations or of God), may bring a high return in human welfare. Just as (thanks to economic advances of the past generation) we no longer see depressions as acts of God or manifestations of the invisible hand, but as controllable human phenomena, so social science may change such views of the international system.[24]

The case for a reordering of priorities rests on the obtrusiveness of the problems, on a conscious normative judgment, and on professional competence in the field of international relations. But there is still another consideration. The reorientation implies a change in emphasis, not a wholesale stampede. There is room enough for a multitude of research topics and methodologies; the case for reorientation does not demand that all other research and theory building be abandoned so that every last scholar and student in the field can address himself to the Indochina conflict or even to the prevention of war. It does, however, mean that far more serious effort must be devoted to the critical problems outlined above. In the past, many studies of these problems have been more informed by wishful thinking, emotional outrage, anecdotal reportage, or policy sanctification than by rigorous analytic techniques. The real challenge is to couple the best scientific methods with application to pressing contemporary needs. This is the heart of the matter, and its consideration requires that we examine some of the past difficulties and present problems in seeking to effect this linkage between professional study and public policy.

There is no lack of obvious and important policy questions that merit scrutiny. But the aim of increased relevance and application of systematic work in international relations to urgent contemporary

---

[23] "Dare We Take the Social Sciences Seriously," *American Behavioral Scientist* 10 (June 1967), in David V. Edwards, *International Political Analysis: Readings* (New York: Holt, 1970), p. 441.
[24] Kenneth Boulding, in Coplin and Kegley, *A Multi-Method Introduction*, pp. 378–79.

problems is not a simple matter. To begin with, the impact of serious international research upon matters affecting defense and foreign policy has been extremely limited. A former bureaucrat in the United States government, with experience in the State Department, National Security Council, Department of Defense, U.S. Air Force, and CIA has commented that he knew of no instance where a foreign service officer or analyst offered any positive comment on a quantitative study. He goes on to attribute the non-use of these studies to unfamiliarity with behavioral methodology, problems of relevance, style and presentation, and poor government-academic relations.[25] This is an often repeated observation or complaint, and an awareness of it can lead to more careful distinctions about the nature of relevant research. That is, while the call for increased relevance has led to heightened emphasis in scientific studies upon subjects related to public policy, much of this work is still highly abstract or else may provide little applicable knowledge. By contrast, research that deals with policy matters in terms of the alternatives that policy planners actually may face is what is needed if professional social scientists are to produce work with any degree of immediate applicability or impact. This has been termed the distinction between "policy research" and "mission research." [26] Thus the first problem is that studies must not merely be relevant, but they must also be addressed in method and substance to practical policy matters—though it should be recognized that both kinds of relevant research have value, since the more abstract policy research can eventually have long-term policy implications even if it is less germane to immediate policy problems.

There is a second and more critical problem in the application of knowledge to policy. It concerns the manner in which this knowledge is actually used or misused. Perhaps the most intractable difficulty so far is that policy analysis may come into play only after decisions have been made, and may provide no more than an

[25] Thomas W. Robinson, "Scholarly Research and Policy Relevance: The Cases of Quantitative International Relations and International Law," The Rand Corporation, April 1971, P–4622, pp. 1–3.

[26] These perceptive distinctions are drawn by Philip M. Burgess, "International Relations Theory: Prospect 1970–1995," paper presented at the Annual Meeting of the American Political Science Association, Los Angeles, California, September 7–11, 1970.

ex post facto rationale or sanctification. An observation by Raymond Tanter is particularly appropriate here:

Foreign policy outcomes may be more a function of bureaucratic bargaining and resource constraints rather than a failure of analysis. . . . Indeed, one former long-range planner in the Johnson and Nixon Administrations claims that most of the analysis comes in *after* policy has been decided. Thus, analysis functions as a tool to substantiate policy views of particular bureaucrats whose policies are already adopted.[27]

Related to this problem is the fact that much of the analysis so far undertaken on the behalf of government tends to be imbued with a more or less static bias, especially when the work is directly or indirectly funded by the government. For example, studies of local conflict in foreign countries have concentrated upon "controllability," and tend to reflect a policy of conflict suppression. Regardless of internal social and political factors, they rarely suggest that anti-status quo activity might be in any way justified.[28] One can easily conceive of situations, for example in Mozambique, Angola, Rhodesia, Haiti, or Greece, where (on the basis of reasonable value judgments) this orientation would be unwise, short-sighted, or even immoral.

Other examples of this tendency toward sanctification of existing policy include a 1967 study undertaken for the United States Department of Defense by a well-known political scientist who concluded that American bombing, artillery and resettlement operations in Vietnam had actually been beneficial to the local population because they resulted in a rapid increase in urbanization, which itself was desirable because urbanization had elsewhere been associated with industrialization, increased living standards, and political development. There was also the abortive Project Camelot, which

---

[27] "Foreign Affairs Analysis: An Activist vs. A Hippie," *International Studies Quarterly* 14 (March 1970): pp. 103–104.

[28] Bernice A. Carroll, "War Termination and Conflict Theory: Value Premises, Theories, and Policies," *The Annals* 392 (November 1970): 27–28. The comments are addressed in particular to a study by Lincoln P. Bloomfield and Amelia C. Leiss, *The Control of Local Conflict* (Washington D.C.: U.S. Government Printing Office, June 1967), which was sponsored by the U.S. Arms Control and Disarmament Agency.

originated in late 1964 through the Special Operations Research Office of the U.S. Army. This involved the largest single social science grant ever given for a project, and its aim was to develop a social systems model for predicting and influencing social change in the developing nations, particularly in Latin America. Its specific objectives were to devise means for determining the potential for civil wars, to identify the actions a government might take "to relieve conditions . . . giving rise to a potential for internal war," and to examine the possibility of establishing a system for obtaining and using the necessary information for doing the above two things.[29] Within a few months, however, a political storm arose in Chile and in the United States over the study and it was abruptly cancelled. While the perspectives and political views of those involved with the study varied widely, the implicit basis for it was one that identified sharp social change anywhere in the underdeveloped world as a social pathology and it was therefore rather one-sided in its implications.[30]

Still another study, with more complicated ramifications, was undertaken by several social scientists affiliated with the Rand Corporation. The object of the study was to assess Viet Cong motivation and morale on behalf of the Office of the Assistant Secretary of Defense for International Security Affairs. In conducting 145 interviews with Viet Cong prisoners of war between July and December 1964, the authors approached their subjects with an explanation that implied they were conducting essentially disinterested social science research:

We usually introduced ourselves as sociology professors studying social conditions in GVN and VC areas and the behavior of men under the stress of revolutionary war.[31]

But in fact the work was directly oriented to governmental policy. The human factors of the insurgency had previously been "under-

---

[29] Quoted in Irving Louis Horowitz, ed., *The Rise and Fall of Project Camelot* (Cambridge, Mass.: M.I.T. Press, 1967), pp. 4–5.
[30] Ibid., p. 44.
[31] John C. Donnell, Guy J. Pauker and Joseph J. Zasloff, "Viet Cong Motivation and Morale in 1964: A Preliminary Report" (Santa Monica, California: The Rand Corporation, RM–4507/3–ISA, March 1965), p. 54. The study was declassified and released for open publication by the Department of Defense in March 1971.

stood only in an impressionistic and intuitive fashion," and the authors realized that this was "bound to affect policy decisions with regard to counterinsurgency." [32] The results of the study were made available during briefings in December 1964 and January 1965 to the United States ambassador and the United States military commander in Saigon and their staffs, to South Vietnamese military staff officers, to the United States Joint Chiefs of Staff, the Defense Intelligence Agency, the State Department, and other high government officials. Subsequently, additional interviewing by Rand staff members took place "to determine, particularly, the precise impact of various tactics and weapons on VC morale." [33]

The outcome and implications of this study are somewhat paradoxical. On the one hand, the authors had undertaken the work at the behest of the Department of Defense with the aim of providing increased knowledge of the Viet Cong, which ultimately could be used to suppress or to kill the enemy more effectively. In this sense we have an apt illustration of the way in which "mission-oriented" research can take its place as a handmaiden to official policy in ways that those who urge "relevance" may not have considered. Yet on the other hand, the study produced findings that indicated that air and artillery strikes on villages tended to help the Viet Cong because the death of innocent peasants outraged their relatives and neighbors and led to increased recruitment of insurgents. They also indicated that casualties did not seem seriously to affect Viet Cong morale.[34] Both these findings implicitly contradicted American military and political policies and perceptions. Perhaps if the results had been more fully appreciated by policy-makers at the time (several months prior to the introduction of full-scale United States bombing of the North and the commitment of combat troops in the South during the spring of 1965), it might have been possible to avoid some of the carnage in Southeast Asia, as well as the disruption within the United States, 50,000 American dead, and tens-of-thousands maimed.

Obviously the call for a closer relationship between political reality and the professional study of international relations has extremely complex ramifications. Not only do the above considerations intrude, but there are other critical concerns involving social

---

[32] Ibid., p. 1.
[33] Ibid., p. v.
[34] Ibid., pp. 45–46 and 74.

science, values, and perceptions. On the question of social science, it is worth noting that some policy-oriented studies that appear to be scientific are nothing of the kind. The work of a number of deterrence theorists has been criticized for its "spurious" air of authority,[35] and Deutsch has identified the way in which "probability" may only serve to cover "glorified belief."[36] On the matter of values, post-behavioralism is not wholly explicit. For example, what if a valid empirical theory of the causes of stability and instability in the underdeveloped world were actually established? What if this knowledge existed so that British policy-makers could have known with some degree of probability whether intervention in Libya against the 1970 radical coup that toppled a traditionalist king could have been swiftly effective (equivalent to the results of some of the French actions to aid friendly governments in recently independent countries of Black Africa), or inconclusive and disastrous (along the lines of the French and American experience in Indochina)? The implications involve matters of political choice that ought to be made as explicit as possible. Certainly this speculation, as well as the cases cited above, should make it quite clear that policy relevance can have very diverse value implications. Finally there is the relationship of applied systematic research to the perceptions of policy-makers. The problem of outmoded or naive images of international reality is critical when it can lead to decisions that may cause large-scale war. Even simple rationality is no small matter.[37] To the extent that international studies may shed more light upon unacknowledged assumptions, displace conspiratorial or Manichean views of international relations, or be conducive

---

[35] Philip Green, *Deadly Logic: The Theory of Nuclear Deterrence* (Columbus, Ohio: Ohio State University Press, 1966), p. xiii. For example, Green argues that some of the work of Herman Kahn is prophetic science fiction rather than scientific analysis (p. 92).

[36] "There is very little difference in our feeling of skepticism when we say that in a certain situation the likelihood of a nuclear attack would seem to us equal to one chance in a thousand, or one in ten thousand, or one in a hundred thousand, but the figures might make a decisive difference to the outcome of the calculation." Introduction to Anatol Rapoport, *Strategy and Conscience* (New York: Schocken, 1969), p. viii.

[37] E.g., Egypt's former Minister of War, Lieutenant General Mohammed Fawzi is said, according to the leading newspaper editor, Mohammed Heykal, to have called upon the spirit of a dead sheik in table-tapping seances in order to ask for advice on the best time for attacking Israel. *New York Times*, June 4, 1971.

in any way toward rationality, they perform a valuable service. Nations may still go to war, but perhaps the danger of their stumbling into it through inadvertence can be reduced.

In this light, the study of "coercive diplomacy" by Alexander George, et al. may be a significant contribution. The authors examine the cases of Laos, the Cuban missile crisis, and the American intervention in Vietnam. They observe that President Kennedy's success in the missile crisis may have produced a set of wrong lessons, which implied that success in other international crises was largely a matter of "national guts." [38] This may have contributed to the disastrous misapplication of the lessons by President Johnson in Vietnam during 1965. The authors' contribution to policy-oriented theory is to identify eight essential conditions for the successful outcome of a coercive strategy; in retrospect, only two of these were present in Vietnam.[39] While the policy and value implications of this study imply the provision of a tool for policy-makers to manipulate as they wish, the components of genuine rationality and prudence that they dictate are at least preferable to the supposedly pragmatic, but actually misleading and ultimately disastrous, lessons absorbed by policy-makers from the Cuban missile crisis.

III. The Possibilities of International Relations Theory

A scientific approach to international politics is at least feasible. Recent work in the field is increasingly able, systematic, and, to a certain extent, has begun to show signs of cumulativeness. The real question is not whether a scientific approach is possible, but what it can tell us and to what uses it can be put. From the standpoint of knowledge and theorizing, simply having such an approach is valuable in itself, for it provides an

---

[38] Alexander L. George, David K. Hall, and William R. Simons, *The Limits of Coercive Diplomacy* (Boston: Little, Brown, 1971), p. xi.
[39] The conditions favoring successful outcome of coercive diplomacy are: strength of U.S. motivation, asymmetry of motivation favoring U.S., clarity of American objectives, sense of urgency to achieve American objective, adequate domestic political support, usable military options, opponent's fear of unacceptable escalation, and clarity concerning the precise terms of settlement. Ibid., p. 227.

ordered perspective for dealing with international reality, and it also determines the questions asked, the relationships examined, and the data selected.

While no one approach dominates the field, the ensemble of them provides an array of techniques and theories that have the potential for helping to edge out conspiratorial and distorted perceptions of reality and thereby aiding the creation of reliable knowledge and the clarification of policy choices and alternatives. It has been an underlying theme here that the approaches of game theory, integration theory, communication theory, theories of power and conflict, and systems theory, as well as others such as decision-making theory, some deterrence theory, and techniques of analysis such as simulation, content analysis, sampling, and the various kinds of aggregate data manipulation offer exciting perspectives for the analysis of international politics. And the theme of this chapter has been that the remaining necessity is to apply the considerable analytic strengths of the behavioral approaches to the compelling political problems of the real world.

It is also the conviction here that the adoption of such an orientation will provide no less of an aid to those who would seek to deal with these compelling realities by reforming or changing the status quo than it does to those who would ignore or perpetuate these problems. Facts, organized into verifiable and reliable knowledge, may have a way of forcing themselves upon the minds of those reluctant to perceive them. If policy-makers are to have their policies and perspectives altered, clear alternatives and informed criticism based on professional expertise must at least be available to them.

To be sure, this is only a part of the picture, since conscious normative choices must also be made. As Deutsch has suggested:

We must choose our values and our risks as a profession. I think we should choose a commitment to truth and to compassion. I believe that we have chosen this commitment and that it will be honored.[40]

Of course the enterprise can still fail. Our analyses, based as they must be on probabilities rather than certainties, cannot cover every conceivable contingency. While we deal with what may be expected to occur a certain percentage of the time, there is ample room for

---

[40] Deutsch, "On Political Theory and Political Action," p. 27.

things that are less probable to occur. If the states of the international system are playing Russian roulette, or to use Hoffmann's metaphor, roulette in the cellar with a nuclear ball, then a statistically improbable occurrence could yet possess cataclysmic significance. If that is not enough of a problem, there remains the difficulty that even the most seemingly verified and systematically gathered information may not in fact be correct; or even when valid, that advice based upon it may be ignored by decision-makers. Yet with all this it must be said that a commitment to professionalism, the urgency of the problems, and certain convincing normative assumptions compel us to make the effort.

Index

164